Opening up
Zephaniah

MICHAEL BENTLEY

DayOne

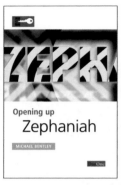

Opening up
Zephaniah

MICHAEL BENTLEY

The Minor Prophets, addressed to a people in transition and spiritual neglect, present God's vital message for today's postmodern culture, facing as it does the potential for major disaster ecologically, financially and spiritually.

Michael Bentley helps both church member and church leader to see how Zephaniah enables us to address contemporary issues in society and church.

The book presents an outstanding balance between a style that is easily read and an experienced study of the context. This commentary is both relevant and challenging, and is an excellent book for use in personal devotion or group study.

Canon Dr Brian Meardon
Vicar of St Michael's Parish Church, Warfield, Bracknell

Say the word 'prophet', and the words 'weird' and 'mad' usually come to mind. Prophets are not popular in the world today, except maybe for a laugh. Michael Bentley's study of the forgotten prophet Zephaniah blows all that away. He shows us that the great purpose of the prophet was not merely to spread gloom and doom and tell us we're all going to die and go to hell, but to point us to God's sending of a Saviour, Jesus Christ, for sinners like you and me. The good news shines from every page. Read it. Study it. Share it. And follow the prophet to the cross of Jesus Christ.

Gordon J. Keddie
Pastor of Southside Reformed Presbyterian Church, Indianapolis, Indiana, USA, and author of numerous books and Bible commentaries

In an increasingly erratic world, where values and standards can change on a whim, solid and sensible advice is desperately required. Michael Bentley's timely book is a breath of fresh air, because it clearly focuses the mind on a valuable portion of God's Word.

Zephaniah is not a dreary text to be consigned to the waste bin of irrelevance, but is a vibrant living call to a world in need. Here is wisdom, correction and warnings that need to be heard.

May God be pleased to give us ears to hear what he is saying as this book is opened up for us.

Clive Anderson
Pastor of the Butts Church, Alton, Hampshire

Contents

© Day One Publications 2008
First printed 2008

ISBN 978–1–84625–111–5

British Library Cataloguing in Publication Data available

Published by Day One Publications
Ryelands Road, Leominster, England, HR6 8NZ
Telephone 01568 613 740   FAX 01568 611 473

email—sales@dayone.co.uk
web site—www.dayone.co.uk

Printed by Gutenberg Press, Malta

Dedication

To my eighth grandchild, Daniel Joseph Underwood, born 4 May 2007.

May he be one in whom the Lord takes 'great delight' (Zeph. 3:17).

List of Bible abbreviations

THE OLD TESTAMENT					
		1 Chr.	1 Chronicles	Dan.	Daniel
		2 Chr.	2 Chronicles	Hosea	Hosea
Gen.	Genesis	Ezra	Ezra	Joel	Joel
Exod.	Exodus	Neh.	Nehemiah	Amos	Amos
Lev.	Leviticus	Esth.	Esther	Obad.	Obadiah
Num.	Numbers	Job	Job	Jonah	Jonah
Deut.	Deuteronomy	Ps.	Psalms	Micah	Micah
Josh.	Joshua	Prov.	Proverbs	Nahum	Nahum
Judg.	Judges	Eccles.	Ecclesiastes	Hab.	Habakkuk
Ruth	Ruth	S. of S.	Song of Solomon	Zeph.	Zephaniah
1 Sam.	1 Samuel	Isa.	Isaiah	Hag.	Haggai
2 Sam.	2 Samuel	Jer.	Jeremiah	Zech.	Zechariah
1 Kings	1 Kings	Lam.	Lamentations	Mal.	Malachi
2 Kings	2 Kings	Ezek.	Ezekiel		

THE NEW TESTAMENT					
		Gal.	Galatians	Heb.	Hebrews
		Eph.	Ephesians	James	James
Matt.	Matthew	Phil.	Philippians	1 Peter	1 Peter
Mark	Mark	Col.	Colossians	2 Peter	2 Peter
Luke	Luke	1 Thes.	1 Thessalonians	1 John	1 John
John	John	2 Thes.	2 Thessalonians	2 John	2 John
Acts	Acts	1 Tim.	1 Timothy	3 John	3 John
Rom.	Romans	2 Tim.	2 Timothy	Jude	Jude
1 Cor.	1 Corinthians	Titus	Titus	Rev.	Revelation
2 Cor.	2 Corinthians	Philem.	Philemon		

Overview

When did you last hear a sermon based on a passage from the prophecy of Zephaniah? This is one of the most neglected books in the whole Bible. It was delivered and written after many years of silence from God. The northern kingdom of Israel, or Ephraim, had already been deported by Assyria, never to return. The prophecy of Zephaniah was to be the last given before Judah, the southern kingdom, was taken away into Babylon for around seventy years of exile.

The prophecy contains many warnings of God's judgement upon a wayward people. Zephaniah has much to say about the 'day of the LORD'. Before him, Amos (in 5:18–20 and 8:9–10), Isaiah (in 2:12; 34:8) and Joel (in 2:2) all spoke about the 'day of the LORD', as did Jeremiah (in ch. 46–51) and Ezekiel (in ch. 7), but Zechariah emphasized this coming day far more than any of the others.

Background and summary

W hen I was young, we had only a few books in the house; they were kept in a small bookcase in the tiny hallway by the front door. There was a two-volume set of the works of David Lloyd-George (Granny was a keen supporter of the old Liberal Party), a dusty copy of the Christmas stories by Charles Dickens and a large-sized purple-covered book called *Sixty Glorious Years*. This was an account of the long reign of Queen Victoria. She reigned for sixty-three years, and, although she died as long ago as 1901, the morality and achievements of the Victorian era still influence Britain today.

Judah in Zephaniah's time

Zephaniah was probably born during another very long reign—that of Manasseh, who was king in Judah for fifty-five years. He had come to the throne at the age of twelve when his godly father Hezekiah died in 687 BC. We are told little about him except this devastating fact: 'He did evil in the eyes of the LORD, following the detestable practices of the nations the LORD had driven out before the Israelites' (2 Kings 21:2). His son Amon became king next, but he continued in the same terrible way until the end of his reign.

Amon's son was Josiah; when he was eight his father was murdered, so he became king at that early age. However, by the time he was sixteen years old (the eighth year of his reign), things had begun to improve. We learn that '[Josiah] began to seek the God of his father David' (2 Chr. 34:3) and that he ordered the removal of the 'altars and the Asherah poles and crushed the idols to powder and cut to pieces all the incense altars throughout Israel' (2 Chr. 34:7).

Next he turned his attention to Jerusalem and gave money to the high priest with instructions to clean up the temple. In 2 Chronicles 34:12–13 we read about the hard work which eventually led to Hilkiah the priest finding 'the Book of the Law of the LORD that had been given through Moses' (v. 14). This precious book was then taken to the king, who gave instructions for it to be read to him.

The effects of God's word

When the king heard God's word, he 'tore his robes' (v. 19), knowing that the Lord's anger was great 'because our fathers have not kept the word of the LORD; they have not acted in accordance with all that is written in this book' (v. 21).

Josiah did not merely remove the worship of false gods: he instituted a reformation in the behaviour and attitude of his people. It is no surprise, then, to read that the first effect of God's word was to bring about a realization of the enormity of the people's sin against the Lord Almighty. At this stage there was little mention of God's love and hope of deliverance; there was only a deep longing in the heart of the king to see repentance in his life and that of his people. He longed for the whole nation to be right with God because he knew blessing would come only if ungodly practices were removed.

Most scholars believe that the Hezekiah mentioned in Zephaniah 1:1 as Zephaniah's great-great-grandfather was the godly king of that name, although it is not certain that this was the case. What we can be sure about is that Josiah's desire for reformation came about around the time that our prophet commenced his ministry. It is likely, then, that Zephaniah grew up knowing the desires for reformation in the royal household; he would also have been aware of the priestly work of the temple.

As it was into the legacy of Manasseh and Amon that Zephaniah was plunged, we are not surprised to find that his prophecy contains many warnings of God's judgement. This awful catalogue continues right up until verse 8 of chapter 3. From then onwards we learn of God's purifying work and the mighty salvation and restoration he has in store for them.

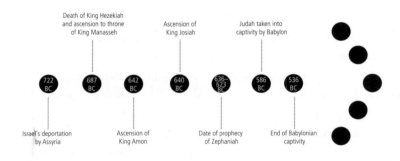

FOR FURTHER STUDY

1. Read about the discovery of the 'Book of the Law' in the temple in 2 Chronicles 34. Note the effect this had on Josiah and the people of Judah.

2. In a concordance, look up the many references to 'the day of the LORD'. Make two lists: one showing those references that speak of God's judgement against sin, and the other those that speak about the coming blessing.

TO THINK ABOUT AND DISCUSS

1. Imagine you are living during the reign of Manasseh and are expected to take part in religious rituals that require you to mix the religion of your heathen neighbours with that of the true God. How would you behave?

2. 'The call to repentance is missing in so much preaching today.' Discuss.

3. When people speak to you about the wickedness and dangers there are in the world today, how can you bring the conversation around to the hope that there is through trusting in the Lord Jesus Christ for salvation?

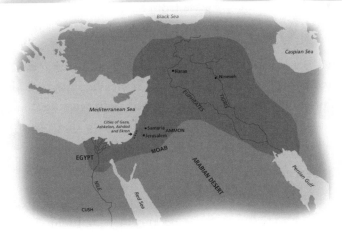

1 Judgement is a reality

(1:1–3)

Jeremiah (1:4), Hosea (1:1), Joel (1:1), Micah (1:1) and Zephaniah (1:1) all start their prophecies in the same way: 'The word of the LORD came'.

We can see that Zephaniah's message did not merely arise from his own thinking; it came from the covenant God of Israel and was therefore authentic as the word of God, aimed specifically at those particular people at that time in their history. It is, however, also a message for us today, because the Bible applies to every people in every age. Sadly, we are no less disobedient to God's voice than were the people of Judah in the 7th century BC.

Judgement announced

The judgement that Zephaniah announces is first directed towards all creatures (vv. 2–3) and then to Judah and the people of Jerusalem (vv. 4–6). The solemnity and urgency of God's action is emphasized by his shout, 'I will sweep away' (stated three times), followed by his stamp of authenticity: 'declares the LORD'.

Men, animals, birds and fish will all be destroyed in this mighty outpouring of God's judgement. It will be like the great flood of Noah's day, but even more destructive. In the days of Noah a family of eight people were saved, but in this final judgement there will be a complete destruction of everyone except the faithful remnant of God's true people (see later comments on 2:7,9 and 3:13).

> Zephaniah's prophecy tells of the complete overthrow of the world and its people; such is the anger of God against them.

Moreover, things will be destroyed in exactly the opposite order to which they were created. We can see this by looking in the first chapter of Genesis: in Genesis 1:20 we read that God created 'fish' then 'birds'. Next came 'animals' (1:25) and finally 'man' (1:26).

Zephaniah's prophecy tells of the complete overthrow of the world and its people; such is the anger of God against them. Mankind, however, is singled out particularly: God will 'cut off man from the face of the earth'. Just as man came from the earth and at death returns to the earth, so at the final judgement he will be 'cut off', that is, completely annihilated.[1]

In the midst of this furore, God says, 'The wicked will

have only heaps of rubble when I cut off man from the face of the earth' (v. 3). The exact meaning of the word translated 'rubble' is uncertain; the New King James Version translates it as 'stumbling blocks' and the English Standard Version has 'idols' (ESV footnote). This word is used to indicate that 'sinful man has managed to twist everything in creation so as to serve his idolatrous purposes'.[2] The final end of those who remain unrepentant is a complete and utter fall.

God's warnings for today

People have heard this message of judgement down through the centuries, and they still need to realize that they are in danger of God's condemnation that is coming upon the whole world. This is why we, like the apostles, preach the gospel of saving grace to everyone who will listen to God's call to turn aside from sin and turn to Christ in repentance and faith. It should be the aim of every church's social and evangelistic activity to bring sinners face to face with the danger of God's judgement and so help them to turn to the only hope of salvation: faith in the Lord Jesus Christ.

The Judeans of Zephaniah's day were probably happy to hear that Zephaniah was calling people to repentance. It was no new message. It is found throughout the whole of the Bible and is one of the major themes of the Old as well as the New Testament. People are sinful, unkind, thoughtless and self-satisfied. They need to turn away from their wicked ways and seek the Lord.

Yet, when Zephaniah started preaching, his message was not received with rapturous applause. On the contrary, it was hated, because instead of addressing it to the heathen around them, it was aimed directly at them.

Today, all people, including church congregations, need to be reminded of the need to repent. Those who have never tasted that the Lord is gracious (Ps. 34:8) need to have their hearts, minds and wills opened to receive the message of God's love, the message that warns them of the danger they are in without Christ and that urges them to 'call on the name of the Lord [and] be saved' (Acts 2:21). Those who have known the presence of the Lord for very many years also need to heed the call to repent and return to the Lord and his ways. Sadly, many Christian people have continued to sin in many ways, not least by gossiping, being jealous of the gifts of others or giving the impression that they are better and more deeply spiritual than others. Those who persist in their unholy ways will be swept away—at least, their boasting will be removed, even though they themselves will be saved, but only as those 'escaping through the flames' (1 Cor. 3:15). This is a very unpopular message, and many preachers today are being urged to drop the old gospel message and only emphasize the fact that God is love and that if we come to him he will meet all of our needs.[3] Yet if we only preach the love of God, we will preach an unbalanced gospel. It is quite wrong and unhelpful to think that we should not preach anything that will challenge people's lives for fear that it will deter them from turning to Christ. The Old Testament prophets pulled no punches when they spoke about God's punishment of evil and disobedience; neither should God's people in these days, as they seek to bring sinners to the foot of the cross in repentance and faith.

FOR FURTHER STUDY

1. What do we learn about the covenant God of Israel from Exodus 6:2–6?

2. Study how the phrase 'cut off' is used in Leviticus 20:3,5–6,17–18; 1 Kings 9:7; and Ezekiel 14:13.

3. Paul wrote in 1 Corinthians 1:23 that the preaching of the cross was a stumbling-block to the Jews. What else does the devil use to deter people from seeking Christ and his salvation (see Jer. 6:21; Ezek. 3:20; Rom. 11:9; and Rev. 2:14)?

TO THINK ABOUT AND DISCUSS

1. In view of a coming final judgement on the earth, how should Christians behave? (See 2 Peter 3:10–12; Matt. 25:13; 1 Thes. 5:6,8.)

2. If you had a lengthy private interview with the prime minister or leader of your country, what advice would you give him or her in the light of God's requirement of the people to obey his laws?

3. What would you say to church leaders who tell you that you should only preach 'God loves you' because to challenge the lifestyle of people would deter them from seeking the Lord?

4. Study the pictures of the church given in 1 Corinthians 3. What does it mean to 'be saved, but only as one escaping through the flames'?

2 Severe Judean pruning

(1:4–6)

Many years after Zephaniah uttered his prophecy, the apostle Peter gave a warning to the believers who had been scattered around the area we now call northern Turkey. It seems that they were in danger of becoming complacent, so he challenged them with these words: 'It is time for judgement to begin with the family of God.' He added, 'And if it begins with us, what will the outcome be for those who do not obey the gospel of God?' (1 Peter 4:17).

The state of the people

Going back to Judah in the 7th century BC, many people considered that they were righteous and godly. They would surely have listened with great interest to Zephaniah's words, but think of the effect his message would have had upon them when they realized that God was speaking directly to them! The Lord did not say, 'Listen carefully, my children; I have a piece of advice that you might like to listen to. See whether you agree with me that it would be a good thing to do.' No; he thundered out with absolute certainty, 'I will stretch out my hand against Judah and against all who live in Jerusalem' (v. 4).

There was nothing vague or mundane about these words. The Lord declared, 'I will stretch out my hand.' Later in the same verse he repeated the words he had used towards the end of verse 3: 'I will cut off ...' Perhaps these Judeans felt like their ancestors who had heard Amos delivering God's judgement upon Damascus, Gaza, Tyre, Edom, Ammon and Moab. They would have been very smug as they learned that God was going to punish their ungodly neighbours—until they realized that he was also condemning Israel and Judah (see Amos 1:3–2:16).

> If the people of Zephaniah's day were sensible and knew their history, they would have understood that God was not beating about the bush: he was being very serious.

If the people of Zephaniah's day were sensible and knew their history, they would have understood that God was not beating about the bush: he was being very serious. This is why the Lord spoke about using his hand. God is spirit and does not have hands or eyes or feet, but, in order for us to understand his actions, the Bible sometimes uses human terms to explain them. We see, then, that just as God's hand is very powerful, his actions will be severe and purposeful.

A religious mixture

The big problem in Judah during the time of Zephaniah was that true religion was mixed with false religion. The Jews were trying to have the best of both worlds. Later on, the Lord Jesus told his disciples, 'No one can serve two masters. Either he will hate the one and love the other, or he will be devoted to the one and despise the other. You cannot serve both God and Money' (Matt. 6:24).

While they had no desire to discard God, they wanted to enjoy the religion of the world around them as well. This had been the continual sin of God's people down through the ages. From the time their forefathers first entered the Promised Land, they wanted to enjoy the immoral worship of Baal and other false religions. They sought to be like their neighbours. They forgot that God's name is holy and that they were his holy people. Instead, they contaminated their worship with falsehoods.

People in New Testament times were no different. Paul had to urge the Corinthians to 'come out' and 'touch no unclean thing' (2 Cor. 6:17), and today God's people are still dabbling with the world and its allurements.

It seems that this part of Zephaniah's prophecy may have been delivered before Josiah's reforms had been carried out, because the people were still able to find places where foreign worship took place, and much later still, in Jeremiah, we find God warning of judgement on the people for continuing to worship the Baals (see Jer. 32:29–30).

Baal worship (v. 4)

Zephaniah knew that even in the heart of the land, in Jerusalem itself, there was 'a remnant of Baal', but God was going to cut this off and completely remove it from their grasp. In 2 Kings 23 we read about some of the action that Josiah took to destroy these heathen places of worship. God was going to cut off every remnant of Baal and even the names of pagan and idolatrous priests. We then find a catalogue of the disgusting behaviour of those who claimed to be God's people.

The priests had been instituted to conduct the worship of God and bring in the means of making it possible to atone for sin; yet these priests, rather than being in the business of removing sin, were actually engaging in wicked practices. God calls them both 'pagan' and 'idolatrous'. But the people did not just engage in Baal worship with its fertility rites and prostitution; they went much further.

Worship of the heavens (v. 5a)

A while ago, my wife and I were on a trip into the outback of Australia and we stayed one night at a cattle station rest house where the nearest neighbours were over 300 kilometres away and the camp generator was switched off at 10 p.m. At 2 a.m. I needed to visit the toilet block. Initially I was very careful where I put my foot, because the area was infested with many highly poisonous snakes, but I forgot all about that as my eyes were drawn upwards. My mouth fell open as I was transfixed by the wonder and glory of the night sky. I had never seen the Milky Way with such clarity and, although the southern night sky was completely foreign to me—apart from the Southern Cross—I just gazed in awe at the vastness of it all.

Having seen that, I can easily understand why heathen people, without knowledge of God, would have been in dread of the immensity of the heavens and the gods who, they believed, dwelt there. It is no surprise that heathen people would have gone up onto their flat roofs and bowed down to worship the starry hosts. Certainly most people who gaze up into the night sky cannot fail to realize that there is someone, somewhere, who is far greater than we are.

Heathens would have worshipped the heavens; but God's people should have known better. Those who want to follow the practices of the world around them, however, will quickly learn to accept the norms of society. Worship of the stars had been closely linked to Baal fertility worship for many generations, and, for Zephaniah, the adoption of this false religion was just one more way of men serving 'created things rather than the Creator' (Rom. 1:25).

Other false gods (v. 5b)

Swearing by Molech (also known as Milcom or Malcham—'king') was additionally detestable. Just as rulers married princesses from neighbouring states to form political alliances, so the Jews adopted the religion of the surrounding nations and attempted to mix it with their own faith. In 1 Kings 11:4–5 we read that even Solomon followed 'Molech the detestable god of the Ammonites'. The worship of this god was especially abhorrent because it required the sacrifice of children. 'The law of Moses demanded the death penalty for everyone who offered his child to Molech (Lev. 18:21; 20:2–5). Nevertheless, King Ahaz burnt his children in the fire (2 Chr. 28:3), and Manasseh did the same (2 Kings 21:6).'[1]

In our day, child sacrifice is still carried on in parts of the world where child prostitution is prevalent and seemingly acceptable to some people; other children are treated like slaves in the home or workplace. Even in very 'respectable' areas, parents today are prone to offer their children to the gods of this age when they

> put more store on their children having membership of many fashionable clubs. They say they do this to give them the best in life; but often it is at the cost of looking after their spiritual future. Jesus himself tells us, 'What good will it be for a man if he gains the whole world, yet forfeits his soul? Or what can a man give in exchange for his soul?' (Matt. 16:26).[2]

God doesn't pay any attention (v. 6)

The last group of people to come under the attack of Zephaniah in this passage are those who have given up on God. There are two kinds of 'believers' in this verse. First are those who 'turn back from following the LORD'. These people probably still carry on going to places of worship at the appropriate times, but in their hearts they have wandered far away from God. They are backsliders, and those who know the truth but deliberately turn their backs upon it are among the most miserable people. They are not like the 'happy pagans'—that is, those who don't know the Lord and therefore are not worried about the judgement that awaits the ungodly. These people here addressed by Zephaniah have made a sincere profession of faith and they know about the requirement to follow the Lord and his ways; yet they turn aside from it. They have forsaken their first love (see Rev. 2:4).

The second group of people mentioned in this verse are those who have never really sought God. They profess to be believers but they have never taken God seriously; they have merely paid lip-service to the Lord. Although they claim conversion, they never really change and grow.

This is a very solemn passage and one to which we should all give heed. We may not bow down to idols of wood and stone, but we might utter phrases such as 'thank heavens' or 'I thank my lucky stars'. God is calling all of us to be sincere in our faith and to turn aside from everything that would keep us from a wholehearted allegiance to the Lord—even close relatives.

For further study ▶

FOR FURTHER STUDY

1. Read the following verses to find out about the use of God's hand, eye, etc: Psalm 36:7; Isaiah 1:15; 1 Peter 3:12; and Acts 11:21.

2. Read 2 Corinthians 6:14–18; 1 John 2:15–17; Revelation 18:4. Which kinds of worldly practices are Christian warned against here?

3. Using an Internet search engine, find out about Baal worship. Then study the following Bible references: Exodus 20:5; Numbers 25:3,5; Jeremiah 1:16; 32:29–30.

TO THINK ABOUT AND DISCUSS

1. How in practice do Christians today try to serve two masters?

2. What do you think Jesus meant when he said, 'Anyone who loves his father or mother more than me is not worthy of me; anyone who loves his son or daughter more than me is not worthy of me' (Matt. 10:37)?

3. 'Sex has become the worship of Baal today; marriage is now merely a means of self-fulfilment, with sex as its sacred rite.' Do you agree? How can marriage be restored to its God-given place in society today?

4. Why should Christians be very wary of becoming involved in New Age culture?

5. We are constantly reminded that we live in a pluralist society. Under which circumstances should Christians be tolerant of other views and the claims of other religions?

3 Let's not disturb God

(1:7–13)

There are so many voices calling for our attention in the world today that there is hardly time to think and certainly little time left to pray about anything. Noise abounds in the streets, and even when we are sitting in the dentist's chair we are likely to be subjected to the incessant sound of musicians.

God's announcement

When the Sovereign Lord speaks concerning the nearness of the day of the Lord, everyone must listen. All must 'be silent' before him, for there is going to be a sacrifice (v. 7). Careful attention must be paid to these events. The prophet proceeds to take his readers on a tour of the city of Jerusalem, starting with the temple and its offerings. Next they journey in their mind's eye to the royal household and finally arrive at the merchant quarters. There are salutary warnings for the people in each of these places, and it is made abundantly clear that no one will escape the gaze of God's all-seeing eyes.

The response of the people

There is a very sharp contrast between God's urgent cry to 'be silent before the Sovereign LORD' (v. 7) and the idle muttering of the people, 'The LORD will do nothing, either good or bad' (v. 12).

Throughout the whole Bible there are numerous warnings addressed to those who pay no attention to God's laws and commands. The Creator and Sustainer of the whole universe is speaking, yet his words fall on minds that regard them as irrelevant. This is especially noticeable with the warnings of the gospel. Christ's call for sinners to repent and turn to him in faith so often falls upon deaf ears.

> The Creator and Sustainer of the whole universe is speaking, yet his words fall on minds that regard them as irrelevant.

However, the Lord does not merely warn: he also gives gracious entreaties to seek him. We find these appeals all the way through the Bible. God's servant, Moses, pleads with the Lord with passion on behalf of the people: 'Please forgive their sin—but if not, then blot me out of the book you have written' (Exod. 32:32); Joel asserts that 'everyone who calls on the name of the LORD will be saved'

(Joel 2:32); and the Lord Jesus himself weeps over Jerusalem: 'O Jerusalem, Jerusalem, you who kill the prophets and stone those sent to you, how often I have longed to gather your children together, as a hen gathers her chicks under her wings', adding with sorrow filling his heart, 'but you were not willing' (Matt. 23:37).

The sacrifice (v. 7)

'The LORD has prepared a sacrifice; he has consecrated those he has invited.' What is this sacrifice Zephaniah speaks of, and who has been called to observe it? The mass of the people would have been excited at the prospect of a huge sacrificial feast. They loved the joyful autumnal festivals. The more spiritual among them, however, would have supposed that something more serious was about to take place—the Lord was going to usher in the final hope of Old Testament religion. They would have assumed that heaven awaited them; yet it was not heaven but hell that was their destination.

History tells us that Judah, God's people, were the sacrifice; they were offered to the nations who descended upon them and carried them away captive. Whether the 'consecrated' ones were God's disobedient people or the nations who pounced upon them is not clear, but it is unnecessary for us to speculate. The 'day of the LORD' was near for Judah because of the people's ungodly behaviour. Zephaniah outlines this in the following verses.

Compromised religion (vv. 8–11)

Zephaniah describes four distinct but overlapping groups

who have not departed from the worship of the Lord but have certainly compromised their religion.

He first speaks about the rulers of the nation: 'I will punish the princes and the king's sons.' We do not know if this refers to the actual children of Josiah, but certainly it was aimed at those who dwelt in the royal court. They had the responsibility of setting an example of godly behaviour to the people, yet they had failed to do so.

Leaders among God's people sometimes fall short of behaving as they should. The praise of the congregation is a fearful temptation which can lead to all manner of sinfulness, such as pride and a love of exerting power over the people of God.

A second group to be punished by the Lord comprised those who dressed in 'foreign clothes'. This would seem to indicate that the ordinary, simple clothing of God's people had been considered to be too dowdy by some of the Judeans, so they copied the fashions and styles of dress of the nations around them. They should have learned that imitating heathen people and their practices can only lead to catastrophe. Way back in the days of the judges, the people had wanted to have a king so that they could be just like the nations around them (1 Sam. 8:6), but their demands had led to the disastrous reign of King Saul.

God always desires basic, wholesome fare for his people, yet human nature has a propensity to want bigger and more elaborate things. Church leaders, too, so often seem bent on building congregations of many hundreds or even thousands. In seeking to achieve those aims, they sometimes forget to put in place the means of caring for the needs of the members of the congregation. Some pastors seem only to have time for the 'new people' and they neglect those who have served the Lord faithfully in their churches for many years. The simple, no-frills presentation of the gospel message does not satisfy the worldly Christian, who wants some of the sharp edges of the faith to be 'toned down' in case they deter non-Christians from 'deciding to follow Christ'.

A third group of worldly believers consists of 'all who avoid stepping on the threshold, who fill the temple of their gods with violence and deceit' (v. 9). It is unclear exactly to what this refers, but it may well allude to a pagan custom that began in the time of Samuel (see 1 Sam. 5:5). What is certain is that the people of Zephaniah's time paid great attention to the detail of their religion but cared little about the requirement to obey God's laws. They were like those in the days of Jesus to whom he said, 'You give a tenth of your spices—mint, dill and cumin. But you have neglected the more important matters of the law—justice, mercy and faithfulness' (Matt. 23:23). The faith of those worldly believers in Zephaniah's time was merely skin deep; they were more concerned to observe outward ceremonies than be holy in their hearts and minds.

> Evangelical Christians can be critical of the behaviour of newly converted believers because they do not comply with the accepted customs of their church.

Evangelical Christians can be critical of the behaviour of newly converted believers because they do not comply with the accepted customs of their church. Sadly, God's people often do not take time to examine whether their practices are carried out 'because we have always done it that way' or because they are clearly based on the teaching of God's Word. We see this, for example, in churches where it is not customary for ladies to attend wearing trousers yet where scant attention is paid to a lady who has newly moved from Asia and has been brought up to believe that it is wrong to expose any part of her legs by wearing a skirt or dress.

The fourth group of those who will be punished are the merchant traders of Jerusalem. Zephaniah is obviously very familiar with the layout of the city. He knows the market district. The Fish Gate was situated in the most vulnerable part of the city; it was not surrounded by hills. The prophet is also familiar with the New Quarter. All of these places were centres of trade and industry. They were also likely to be the seat of much corruption and dishonesty, where, as always, the poor were the losers.

God warns Judah that on the day of the Lord these areas will be utterly destroyed and the livelihood of the people will vanish, causing them to utter a great cry of anguish. One of the reasons for this is because God will not be mocked. He will remove all injustice and selfishness on that day. Just as 'power corrupts and absolute power corrupts absolutely', to use Lord Acton's famous saying, so the love of money proves to be the root of all evil (1 Tim. 6:10). There is a danger that in some churches the deacons could be likened to these traders. Their task is to look after the money and fabric of the church buildings, but occasionally their love of power can overwhelm them and they have been known to use that to ensure their purposes are achieved.

Complacent religion (vv. 12–13)

But God will not allow these things to continue. No one will escape his searching eye. He will 'search Jerusalem with lamps' so that he can see into all of the dark corners of the city. Yet the Lord does not need physical lights to discover the darkness of our minds and hearts. He has all-seeing eyes from which nothing can be hidden. Zephaniah's message is that, before long, the Babylonians will come and drag people from their houses and wherever they try to hide from the invading forces.

The Lord's objective here was not merely to seek out the ungodly; he was searching for complacent believers, too. These people wanted to be identified as the people of God, yet they were idle and ignored the responsibilities that are required of true followers of God. They were like wine that had been left in its jar to allow the sediment to sink to the bottom, and so become cloudy, instead of continually being poured from one jar to another so that the dregs can be siphoned off. These citizens had become 'settled in their indifference to God'[1] and had no real concern except to take life easy. They were like the people of Amos's time, who were 'at ease in Zion' (Amos 6:1, AV). Certainly they were not worried, because they believed that 'the LORD will do nothing, either good or bad' (v. 12).

They were like many in the world today. Such people care nothing for the Lord and his glory, yet they are proud to live in 'a Christian country' and insist that they are 'godly people who live by the Christian ethic'. They think, 'I will trust and not be afraid' (see Isa. 12:2). However, the Lord says to such people, 'Their wealth will be plundered, their houses demolished. They will build houses but not live in them; they will plant vineyards but not drink the wine' (v. 13). All of these, and many more, will discover that, when the day of the Lord finally comes, their 'couldn't care less' attitude will be smashed to the ground.

1. Read Psalm 37:7; Isaiah 41:1; Habakkuk 2:20; Zechariah 2:13. Note the great importance that the Bible places on the need to be silent before the Lord.
2. What do we learn from the following passages about the strength of the 'eyes' of the Lord: Daniel 10:6; Revelation 1:14; 2:18; 19:12?
3. Study the following entreaties of the Lord to return to him: Deuteronomy 4:29; Isaiah 55:3; Amos 4:6–11; 5:4; Jeremiah 3:6–10; 29:13. What do they tell us about the character of God?

TO THINK ABOUT AND DISCUSS

1. How important is a reverent, thoughtful approach to God in prayer? Under what kinds of circumstances is a hurried approach permissible?
2. How much time and effort should we give to seeking to win a loved one to Christ?
3. The people were chastised for wearing 'foreign clothes'. What dangers are there for Christians who adopt worldly strategies in their efforts to win people for Christ?
4. What criteria should be used by a Christian businessman or woman in the allocation of time for work, family and the Lord's work?

4 Sin is dangerous

(1:14–18)

The prophet now launches into a tirade of doom. Just as the opening four notes of Beethoven's Fifth Symphony hammer out their menacing sound all the way through its first movement, so 'that day' thunders through this section of Zephaniah's prophecy with horrendous impact—'The great day of the LORD is near … The cry on the day of the LORD …, (v. 14).

'That day will be a day of wrath, a day of distress … a day of clouds' (v. 15), a day of 'trumpet and battle cry' (v. 16) and, ultimately, 'the day of the LORD's wrath' (v. 18). The repeated emphasis on the word 'day' causes it to penetrate deeper into our minds and souls every time we hear it.

Although the inhabitants of Jerusalem were going to experience something like the dreadful calamity depicted here, the fullest impact of God's wrath will not be launched against a city; it will be unleashed upon the whole world. Yet, unlike man's 'justice', there will be nothing unfair or unreasonable about God's punishment. The people are left in no doubt about the reason for it. These things will come upon them for one reason only: 'because they have sinned against the LORD' (v. 17). Here, as elsewhere in the Bible, we see that God will not tolerate disobedience of his law and word.

The nearness of that day

Josiah had sought to rid the land of the false religions of Baal and other iniquities, and his efforts had bought time for the people. The Lord told him,

> Because your heart was responsive and you humbled yourself before the LORD when you heard what I have spoken against this place and its people, that they would become accursed and laid waste, and because you tore your robes and wept in my presence, I have heard you ... Therefore I will gather you to your fathers, and you will be buried in peace. Your eyes will not see all the disaster I am going to bring on this place (2 Kings 22:19–20).

Josiah's actions had achieved an extra thirty-six years' grace for them. Not until he had died would the dreadful Babylonian army finally enter Jerusalem and wreak havoc upon the city, its temple and its people.

The people were not to relax, however, because 'the great day of the LORD is near—near and coming quickly' (v. 14). It is a big temptation to think that there is plenty of time before we need to make amends for our sins. Jesus told his disciples, 'Do you not say, "Four months more and then the harvest"? I tell you, open your eyes and look at the fields! They are ripe for harvest' (John 4:35). The sins of the world are so great that the Grim Reaper will soon come and cut through the pride and selfishness of mankind and reap the harvest he has promised at the end of the age. We should not be content to wait and see what will happen because, like a thief, the day of the Lord will come unexpectedly (2 Peter 3:10), and no one will be able to escape God's judgement (Rom. 2:3).

> The sins of the world are so great that the Grim Reaper will soon come and cut through the pride and selfishness of mankind and reap the harvest he has promised at the end of the age.

We should not be like those of Peter's day who said, 'Where is this "coming" he promised? Ever since our fathers died, everything goes on as it has since the beginning of creation' (2 Peter 3:4). Of course, those first-century people conveniently forgot the Flood that destroyed everything except for those beings that were safe in God's ark. They needed to remember that 'by the same word the present heavens and earth are reserved for fire, being kept for the day of judgement and destruction of ungodly men' (2 Peter 3:7)—and we today need to remember that, too.

Judgement upon sin will come, and it will soon be upon us. No believer should feel complacent because of the knowledge that he or she has been saved with God's eternal salvation and that 'no one can snatch [him or her] out of [God's] hand' (John 10:28). We must heed Peter's warning: 'It is time for judgement to begin with the family of God; and if it begins with us, what will the outcome be for those who do not obey the gospel of God?' (1 Peter 4:17).

Our great task is to warn people of the danger they are in without Christ. The 'emerging church' movement may urge us to concentrate on telling people about God's love for them, but if we fail to warn them of the need to repent of their sin and believe the gospel, they will die—and God will hold us accountable (see Ezek. 33:8).

The effects of that day

The prophet commands the people to 'Listen!' This is no vague request, but rather is designed to seize their full attention so that they will listen very carefully to the words of the Lord.

The disaster that will descend upon the people on that great day of the Lord will cause an anguished cry to go up from the city; the cry will be very bitter and will be mingled with the shouting of the soldiers bringing great distress upon everyone. All kinds of disasters, such as cropfailure, attacks from heathen neighbours and fierce weather, will be as nothing in comparison with the blackness and ruin that will be wrought upon the people of Jerusalem on the day of their conquest by the Babylonians. Furthermore, that will be as nothing in comparison with the judgement that God will bring upon the whole world at the end times.

This scene is one that could be depicted in a multimedia

presentation to a congregation. The people would see the flashing of the chariots and hear the shouts of the conquerors mingled with the agony of the people of Jerusalem as their city is trashed. Even then, the smell of battle would be missing—but it can be imagined as we read this graphic account of destruction.

Zephaniah goes on to illustrate the hopelessness of the people by telling us that 'they will walk like blind men' and that 'their blood will be poured out like dust and their entrails like filth'. They will not know what to do, and all of them, from the greatest to the least, will be in the same situation.

People always want to do something to make matters appear to be better than they really are. In the stories of the kings in the Old Testament, an enemy was frequently 'bought off' by the payment of tribute money, but here we are told that 'Neither their silver nor their gold will be able to save them' (v. 18). People still believe that money can solve their problems, but when we see how most billionaires behave, we realize that money in itself does not bring happiness or even health.

There is nothing that can be done to escape 'the fire' of God's jealousy, which will consume the whole world and make a sudden end of it. Revelation 6:15–17 describes the day of God's wrath in graphic detail:

> The kings of the earth, the princes, the generals, the rich, the mighty, and every slave and every free man hid in caves and among the rocks of the mountains. They called to the mountains and the rocks, 'Fall on us and hide us from the face of him who sits on the throne and from the wrath of the Lamb!

For the great day of their wrath has come, and who can stand?'
So what can people do to relieve their discomfort? Where can
anyone go to escape from the anger of divine justice? Just as
the only safety for Noah and his family was to go inside the
ark, so the only place where we can hide from God's
vengeance is the blood of Christ, because 'the blood of Jesus,
[God's] son, purifies us from all sin' (1 John 1:7). The only
place of shelter is the Rock, Christ Jesus, as Augustus Toplady
summed it up in his lovely hymn written around 1775:

Not the labour of my hands
Can fulfil thy law's demands;
Could my zeal no respite know,
Could my tears for ever flow,
All for sin could not atone;
Thou must save, and thou alone.

Nothing in my hand I bring,
Simply to thy cross I cling;
Naked, come to thee for dress;
Helpless, look to thee for grace;
Foul, I to the fountain fly;
Wash me, Saviour, or I die.

While I draw this fleeting breath,
When my eyelids close in death,
When I soar to worlds unknown,
See thee on thy judgement throne,
Rock of Ages, cleft for me,
Let me hide myself in thee.

For further study ▶

42

FOR FURTHER STUDY

1. Consider what God says about that great 'day': Psalm 90:3–6; Obadiah 15 and 2 Peter 3:8.
What will be the effects of God's wrath on that day? See Isaiah 13:9,13; Hosea 5:10; Joel 2:31 and Matthew 24:29.
2. What are some of the marks that indicate that man has fallen far short of God's standard? See Jeremiah 6:13–16 and Romans 1:21–23.
3. How should we prepare for the day of God's wrath? See 1 Thessalonians 5:1–11 and 2 Peter 3:11–12.

TO THINK ABOUT AND DISCUSS

1. What indications are there in our day that the Lord will come with judgement on an unrepentant world?
2. How should Christian people act when they are aware of the danger that awaits a sinful world?
3. How would you reason with a person who believes that he or she can appease God's wrath through good works and generosity? (See Isa. 1:10–17; Jer. 7:8–15; Micah 6:6–8 and Acts 8:18–23.)

5 A glimmer of hope

(2:1–3)

The prophet now moves his attention back to Jerusalem and addresses the people with these surprising words: 'O shameful nation'. This must have been an appalling shock for them.

They had assumed that all was well, but here was the Lord calling his own people a nation, and a shameful nation at that! How could he do that when they were his chosen covenant people whom he had rescued from Egyptian slavery and brought through the desert into this Promised Land? Surely it was all the ungodly nations around them that deserved God's judgement, not the people of Judah! But when the Lord speaks, everyone should listen to the things that he has to say.

This is why so many Christian people go astray in these days: they do not pay attention to the Word of God. They listen to people's ideas and fanciful 'prophecies' from those who claim to speak for the Lord, but they are not so quick to heed the clear teaching of Scripture.

Attention, thoughtless nation (vv. 1–2)

The first thing the Lord urges the people to do is 'gather together'. This is such an urgent matter that he says it twice. He does not here speak to individuals, as he had spoken to Zephaniah and others in the past. Rather he addresses them as a group—a nation.

The people would have had no difficulty understanding why the Lord used the word 'gather'. This was what happened to the stubble at the end of the harvest: those worthless, short, sharp ends of the corn stalks were always carefully collected and cast into the fire to be consumed. The people of Judah had been content, thinking that they were secure; they believed that they would be allowed to carry on living undisturbed by man or God. They assumed that the Lord would leave them to their own devices. They would have regularly stated, 'The LORD will do nothing, either good or bad' (1:12).

Yet the words of Zephaniah continued to carry urgency. We can see this in his use of the word 'before':

Gather together, gather together,

O shameful nation,

before the appointed time arrives

and that day sweeps on like chaff,

before the fierce anger of the LORD comes upon you,

before the day of the LORD's wrath comes upon you [italics added].

In other words, if there was to be any hope for them, they needed to act '*before* the appointed time'.

Rather than just being left to themselves, God's judgement would certainly come, and it would arrive at the appointed time; nothing would be able to hinder or divert its approach. It would not be like human anger; it would be 'the fierce anger of the LORD'. Again the prophet referred to 'the day'; it would be 'the day of the LORD's wrath'. That day would certainly sweep them like chaff.

Judah was an agricultural land, and everyone knew that, when the crops were gathered, the ears of corn had to be winnowed or threshed. This meant beating the stalks of corn on the ground or against a rock and so releasing the kernels which were used to make flour. As the heavier corn dropped to the ground, the lightweight husks, the chaff, would be taken away in the wind, like so much useless dust. That is exactly how God viewed worthless Judah. Because they had no value, they were going to be blown away by the wind of God's judgement, that is, by the Babylonians.

I wonder what effect Zephaniah's words had upon the people. I can still remember the days following the end of the Second World War; everyone living in Britain was tense. Our newspapers constantly reminded us of the huge numbers of nuclear warheads that were aimed in our direction from the Soviet-occupied countries of Eastern Europe. We were scared, just as we had been during the threat of Nazi invasion a few years earlier, but we did nothing because we felt that the country was being looked after by our government.

Some people believed that God had provided a miraculous deliverance of our nation in the days of the Dunkirk evacuation, when the seas were remarkably calm, allowing 338,226 soldiers to be lifted off the beaches. Therefore, to the minds of some, what the Lord had done for Britain in 1940 he would continue to do. Complacency is a disease that was not confined to Judah in the 7th century BC.

Ingratitude is something we deplore in children; we are horrified when parents do not insist that their little ones say 'thank you' for presents that are given to them. Yet are we, as God's people, any better? We ought to live our lives in humble gratitude to God for all his mercies to us in saving us and holding back his hand of judgement upon our sinful nation.

God's amazing grace (v. 3)

With such announcements of impending judgement upon the people, we are surprised to read that such sinful people were given a small glimmer of hope, if only they would act upon it.

But first a change had to take place. The people needed to alter their thinking and then their actions. Once, Jesus amazed the people by taking a little child and standing him among them. He told them, 'Unless you change and become like little children, you will never enter the kingdom of heaven' (Matt. 18:3). This was a revolutionary thought to them; children were to be seen and not heard, yet here was Jesus saying that God's people must become like children. He meant that they must humble themselves and trust their father—just as a little child, crossing a busy road, will look straight ahead and ignore the noisy traffic if his or her hand is held firmly by Grandad. Just as that little child trusts Grandad, so we are required to trust our heavenly father.

The people of Jerusalem had nothing to offer to God to

cause him to divert his judgement upon them, yet there was one thing they could do. They could 'Seek the LORD', but this would require humility. Those who are proud will see no need to seek the Lord; they will prefer to manage things in their own strength. They will have no wish to humble themselves under God's mighty hand (1 Peter 5:6). They will see this as 'weakness'.

Yet God requires humility of his people. Here in our passage he says that perhaps they will be safe if they humbly seek the Lord. This is what the Lord requires of us. Through the prophet Micah we learn, '[God] has showed you, O man, what is good. And what does the LORD require of you? To act justly and to love mercy and to walk humbly with your God' (Micah 6:8).

> If they were to have any hope of being sheltered from the day of God's judgement, they needed to 'seek righteousness' and 'humility'.

If they were to have any hope of being sheltered from the day of God's judgement, they needed to 'seek righteousness' and 'humility'. These qualities should be at the centre of our lives. To those who had been worrying about how to obtain the necessities of life the Lord Jesus Christ himself said, 'Seek first his kingdom and his righteousness, and all these things will be given to you as well' (Matt. 6:33). There is comfort too in the words of James: 'God opposes the proud but gives grace to the humble' (James 4:6).

What applied to Jerusalem in the 7th century BC is still true for us today. Self-aggrandizement and popularity are what many seek now, yet it is the humble who will succeed, because they have nothing of which they can boast. It is not their own efforts that have saved them or granted them prosperity. Certainly we are all required to work hard and earn our livings, but God honours those who honour him and obey his word. It will be the meek who will 'inherit the earth' (Matt. 5:4).

Spiritual success is not like putting a coin in a slot machine and obtaining a bar of chocolate. Just as those of Jerusalem could not earn their safety through their own efforts, neither can we. All of us are in the hands of God. Our salvation is dependent solely upon his grace and mercy. He never says to us that, if we observe certain requirements, he will reward us in that measure. To Jerusalem he said, 'Seek the LORD, all you humble of the land, you who do what he commands. Seek righteousness, seek humility; perhaps you will be sheltered on the day of the LORD's anger.'

The little word 'perhaps' is one of grace, not reward. Our only hope is to cast ourselves entirely upon the mercy of God. We must live for him knowing that we are utterly dependent on his mercy. We have no claim on him, only on his mercy.

FOR FURTHER STUDY

1. Investigate the use of the word 'chaff' in the Bible. How can we ensure that our lives are of more value than this waste substance? (See Ps. 1:4; Isa. 17:13; Dan. 2:35; Hosea 13:3.)

2. Read the following passages: 2 Samuel 12:1–7; Amos 3:14–15; Haggai 1:5,7; 2:14–15,18. Imagine the horror God's people felt when they realized that all was not well with them.

3. Note God's gracious calls to sinful people to seek him and rejoice in his goodness: Psalm 22:26; Amos 5:6; Isaiah 55:6–7; Matthew 7:7–8.

4. Read the following verses: Ephesians 4:2; Philippians 2:3; Colossians 3:12; 1 Peter 5:5–6; Romans 12:16; James 1:21; Luke 14:10; Proverbs 12:9; 16:19. What does God say about humility?

TO THINK ABOUT AND DISCUSS

1. When did you last show your gratitude to the Lord for saving and sustaining you? What can you do to show your continual love for the Lord? How can you encourage others to live in the same spirit of praise and thanksgiving?

2. Discuss this statement: 'It is unfair of God to save wicked people who believe in Jesus yet condemn those who have lived a good, clean "Christian" life but have never felt the need of God.'

6 Trouble all around

(2:4–12)

When Christian people receive special blessing from the Lord, everyone benefits, even though no one deserves it. In a similar way, when God's people come under his chastening hand, those around are also likely to suffer; but in this case, they do deserve it, because of their unrepentant hearts.

The second half of chapter 2 of Zephaniah's prophecy gives us some clear hints of the tribulation that is going to come upon the nations around Judah. 'Zephaniah uses the example of what awaits the surrounding nations as a warning, giving Judah good reason to repent, as he had warned them to do ([2:]1–3).'[1] We in our day should also take notice of the admonitions of God's Word. God is a God of love, but he also demands justice and righteousness in and from his people.

As we look at this section of the prophecy, we are directed to consider those who lived all around Jerusalem—to the west, the east, the south and the north—as the prophet speaks about their punishment.

Places to the west (vv. 4–7)

Gaza, Ashkelon, Ashdod and Ekron are all mentioned. These cities are where the Philistines once ruled supremely. They are addressed in geographical order, starting with Gaza in the south and travelling northwards. The one omission from this list is Gath, the home of Goliath and the city where the ark of the covenant was once housed (1 Sam. 5:8). The reason why Gath was left out of this condemnation may be because, under King Uzziah's rule, Judah 'went to war against the Philistines and broke down the walls of Gath' (2 Chr. 26:6); perhaps it was still under Judean control.

Notice the words that are used to describe the consequences of the Philistines' sinfulness: Gaza will be 'abandoned'; Ashkelon, 'left in ruins'; Ashdod, 'emptied'; Ekron, 'uprooted'; and the Kerethite people will be destroyed. This indicates the completeness of God's judgement upon them. It will be sudden and unexpected (v. 4), total (v. 5) and final (v. 9). No one will be spared.

The message for these cities and for Jerusalem is the same for us in our day. The time is coming when God will suddenly avenge sinners. They and we have been warned.

Notice the details. Ashdod would be emptied at midday. This would be either because the attack would come during the hottest part of the day, when everyone was relaxed and enjoying a siesta, or maybe because the conquest would be swift and easy and would only take part of a day to succeed.

Twice we are told that the Kerethites lived by the sea (vv. 5–6); tradition says that these were people who originated from the island of Cyprus. This once well-populated land was going to be destroyed, and instead of having houses it would be 'a place for shepherds and sheep pens'. For these people, and, indeed, all who disobey the Lord and his word, it is devastating to learn that 'the LORD is against [them]' (v. 5).

> Here once again is evidence of God's grace in action. Although destruction will come upon the people of Judah, there will be a small number who will survive.

Romans 8:31 asks, 'If God is for us, who can be against us?' The answer is that no one can defeat us if the God of all the earth is with us. With his presence we are safe for evermore; but how dreadful for those who will learn that this same Lord is 'against' them! What escape is there for them? They are off course and helpless.

However, in verses 7 and 9 we read of a glimmer of hope; all may not be lost. In fact, there will be a 'remnant of the house of Judah'. Here once again is evidence of God's grace in action. Although destruction will come upon the people of Judah, there will be a small number who will survive. Moreover, they will not just be left hanging on 'by the skin of their teeth'; they will be well provided for: 'In the evening they will lie down [in peace]' and 'The LORD their God will care for them [and] restore their fortunes' (v. 7). How wonderful is the grace and mercy of our God in giving us the assurance of his presence and care so that, whatever happens to us, we know that all will be well!

God does not behave like men; he is not vindictive. He holds out the hand of love to all who will turn to him and receive his mercy. The same offer still stands today: the vilest sinner has but to stretch out the hand of faith (even though it is empty of anything of value) and cling to the cross of Christ. He or she will then find forgiveness and eternal life. Now we see that the 'perhaps' of 2:3 has manifested itself in the assurance that there will be a remnant of the godly who will be saved on the day of destruction.

Places to the east (vv. 8–11)

We now move into the area where God once rained down his judgement on the wicked cities of Sodom and Gomorrah (Gen. 18:20–21). Abraham tells us that the Lord did what was right when he poured out his righteous anger upon the inhabitants of those cities (Gen. 18:25). Although Lot had been living in Sodom and escaped from its annihilation, the nations of Moab and Ammon sprang from incestuous relationships between him and his daughters (Gen. 19:30–38). These two nations were, therefore, blood relations of Judah, yet down through the centuries they had been a constant irritation to God's people. We are horrified when we read in 2:8 of the 'insults' of Moab and the 'taunts', 'insults' and 'threats' of Ammon against Judah, the nation whom God describes as 'my people'.

Because of the behaviour of Moab and Ammon, God

condemns them. He makes a solemn declaration: 'as surely as I live … Moab will become like Sodom, the Ammonites like Gomorrah—a place of weeds and salt pits, a wasteland for ever' (v. 9). This will be the fulfilment of the curses pronounced in Deuteronomy 29:23: 'The whole land will be a burning waste of salt and sulphur—nothing planted, nothing sprouting, no vegetation growing on it.'

Then we are told that the remnant of God's people 'will plunder them; the survivors of my nation will inherit their land'. This will be their reward because they have long endured insults and mocking (v. 10) and also because Moab and Ammon have been filled with pride (Num. 22–25; Judg. 10–11; Isa. 16:6; Jer. 48:29).

Christian people often have to endure unjust treatment. In Britain there are increasing signs that those who bear witness to the Bible's teaching on Christian marriage and speak against issues such as same-sex unions will have to suffer as a consequence. We should not be surprised by these things, because the Lord Jesus Christ tells us that 'In this world you will have trouble' (John 16:33), adding, for our comfort, 'But take heart! I have overcome the world.'

John Bunyan must often have wondered how much longer he would have to stay in Bedford gaol while his wife suffered at home without him, yet eventually the day came when he was released. Because of his suffering 'for righteousness' sake' (Matt. 5:10, AV), we all have benefited through his labours on *The Pilgrim's Progress* and other books that he wrote while in prison.

We should also be encouraged because, just as the remnant of Judah were blessed through their added inheritance, so we too will eventually gain our reward because we have been faithful to our high calling in Christ Jesus (Phil. 3:14).

Verse 11 promises that the gospel will be universal in its application. One day, all false gods will be destroyed and 'The nations on every shore will worship [the Lord]'. Isaiah tells us that there is a day coming when 'Many peoples will come and say, "Come, let us go up to the mountain of the LORD, to the house of the God of Jacob"' (Isa. 2:3; Micah 4:1–3), and Zephaniah makes it clear that 'the nations' will worship him, 'every one in its own land' (v. 11).

Places to the south (v. 12)

From Philistia in the west and Moab and Ammon to the east, the prophet now turns his hearers' and readers' attention to the south. Here we have the shortest of these judgements— that against Cush. Cush was Ethiopia, the Nubian kingdom. It 'stretched south from Aswan, the first cataract of the Nile, to the Nile's junction near modern Khartoum'.[2] This judgement is probably against Egypt as a whole and the lands to the south.

Herodotus stated concerning Ethiopia, 'Its people are of great size and beauty, and long-lived',[3] but this did not deter the one true and living God. With simple words, the Lord declared, 'You too, O Cushites, will be slain by my sword.' Certainly Cambyses II of Persia defeated Egypt in 525 BC,[4] and we know that the Lord did, and still can, use heathen powers to carry out his decrees.

For further study ▶

FOR FURTHER STUDY

1. Read Joshua 13:3; Judges 3:3; and Amos 1:6,8. Find out more about the history of the Philistine cities using encyclopaedias and the Internet.

2. Study the theme of 'the remnant' in Isaiah (see 10:20–22; 11:11; 37:30–32; and also its suggestion at Isaiah's call to be a prophet in 6:13).

3. What does God say about the Moabites and the Ammonites in Isaiah 15–16; Jeremiah 48; 49:1–6; Ezekiel 25:1–11; Amos 1:13–2:3?

TO THINK ABOUT AND DISCUSS

1. What should we do when we realize that the word of the Lord is against us? (See Zeph. 2:5; Lev. 26:14–45; Amos 3:1.)

2. How will God's judgement on sinners be like that on Sodom and Gomorrah? (See Gen. 18:20; Isa. 1:9; Amos 4:11; Matt. 10:15; 2 Peter 2:6.)

3. Why is pride such a terrible sin? What lies at the heart of the boastful attitude that makes communion with God impossible? (See Isa. 16:6; Jer. 48:29; Rom. 1:28–31.)

4. On what basis can we sing, 'Jesus shall reign where'er the sun does his successive journeys run; his kingdom stretch from shore to shore, till moons shall wax and wane no more' (Isaac Watts)? (See Isa. 19:19,21,23; Mal. 1:11; John 4:21–23; 2 Peter 3:13; Rev. 21:1–4.)

7 Doom to the dreaded Assyria

(2:13–15)

Having mentioned the nations which immediately surround Judah, the Lord now directs his people to consider that most powerful nation of the day: Assyria. For some 400 years, this empire had dominated the whole area around it; it had wrought havoc on its neighbours, including Judah. The terrible cruelty it inflicted on its captured enemies was as bad as, if not worse than, any inflicted by the Nazi regime of Adolf Hitler.

The danger in the north

The mighty empire of Assyria lay to the north and north-east of Judah. It expanded until it conquered the lands all the way down the Fertile Crescent between the mighty Tigris and

58

Euphrates rivers. Nations trembled before it, and its proud boast was that its capital, Nineveh, was a 'carefree city that lived in safety' (v. 15). This claim could be made because no nation would dare to stand against it. Its thirty-metre-high walls were so thick that three chariots could go abreast on them, and the 1,500 towers on the wall were used to house watchmen.

In its exalted state, this city declared, with great boldness, 'I am, and there is none besides me' (v. 15). As with Moab and Ammon (v. 10), pride gripped Assyria. With great pomp it held up its head, little realizing that soon it would fall, just as the statue of Saddam Hussein fell before the Baghdad crowds in 2003.

> No one can challenge the Lord of the universe and hope to escape his judgements.

No one can challenge the Lord of the universe and hope to escape his judgements. Through Isaiah, that same God thunders out with infinitely greater power, 'I am the LORD, and there is no other' (Isa. 45:5). Those who challenge the Lord and his people will be defeated in the end. Throughout the world today, there are thousands who deny the existence or power of the Lord, but, like Nineveh, they will soon be defeated.

A few years ago, my wife and I were in a hot air balloon near the Valley of the Kings in Egypt. We saw the sun rise and light up the Colossi of Memnon—two 18-metre-tall statues of Pharaoh Amenhotep III standing proudly over the whole land, as they have done for the past 3,400 years. Nearby lies half-buried in the sand the partial stone head of another pharaoh. It was this broken head that inspired Shelley to write his poem 'Ozymandias', in which the plinth of Ozymandias boasts, 'My name is Ozymandias, King of Kings: Look on my works, ye Mighty, and despair!' Then, as the imagination of Shelley observes it, its 'glory' becomes as insignificant as a shattered and mutilated stone. Shelley ended his poem by saying, 'Nothing beside remains. Round the decay of that colossal wreck, boundless and bare, The lone and level sands stretch far away.'[1] History knows nothing of this mighty Ozymandias, and so it will be for all those who seek to exalt themselves above the authority of the Lord God Almighty.

It was the same with once-proud Nineveh. That city was invaded and overthrown by the Babylonians, the Medes and the Scythians. Ezekiel 32:22–23 gives some details of this. Earlier, in the days of Jonah, we learn that the people of Nineveh repented of their sin, but they quickly fell back into their old sinful ways again, as is recorded in Nahum 2–3. Repentance must be genuine and permanent, otherwise it has no lasting value. Nearly two centuries after Nineveh was destroyed, the Greek historian Xenophon could find no trace of it.[2]

As happened with Nineveh, 'destruction will ultimately come to all who put their trust in any defence other than the Lord God Almighty. All who seek joy in anyone, or anything, other than in the Lord will be sadly disillusioned. Everyone who plots evil against the Lord and counsels wickedness will be utterly destroyed.'[3]

Zephaniah tells us, '[The Lord] will stretch out his hand

against the north and destroy Assyria' (v. 13). The mighty hand of Assyria, powerful as it is, will be no match for God, the Lord of the universe (who will destroy all gods—2:11). The once-thriving city of human activity will become utterly desolate and as dry as the desert. Instead of people, animals—both wild and domestic—will use Nineveh's ruins for their homes. Some of these animals are those that Leviticus 11 declares to be unclean: Nineveh's ruins will be unclean and forsaken.

Where ruined pillars are left standing, their once-ornate capitals on the tops will provide roosting-places for owls; rubble will fill the doorways which once gave access to homes. Even the strong but formerly hidden cedar beams will be exposed to the elements. The prophet cries out, 'What a ruin she has become, a lair for wild beasts!' (v. 15).

Verse 13 starts by telling us that God will stretch out his hand against the city, and verse 15 ends by stating that those who pass by the ruins will 'scoff and shake their fists'. Once-proud and mighty Assyria will become a place of derision, and such will be the end of all those seeking to rise above the Lord and usurp his authority.

What a salutary lesson this is for Christian people today! Zephaniah told the people of Jerusalem about the destruction God was going to bring upon their neighbours not so that the people of Judah could gloat over them, but in order that they themselves would take careful note and be humbled.

Leaders of churches can so easily feel self-sufficient when all is going well, congregations are increasing and people are constantly thanking and praising them for their preaching abilities and acts of service. However, they should regularly remind themselves that, at best, they are 'only servants' of Christ and his people (2 Cor. 3:5). Pride is a disease that spreads quietly but rapidly until it has gained the victory over those who had formerly walked humbly with their God.

For further study ▶

FOR FURTHER STUDY

1. Nineveh said, 'I am, and there is none besides me' (v. 15). Note what the Lord said would happen to this once-proud city (vv. 13–15), and take heed to the following warnings against pride: Proverbs 21:24; Romans 12:3; Galatians 6:3; Romans 11:20; James 4:6; 1 Peter 5:5.

2. Compare the devastation of Nineveh in Zephaniah 2:13–15 with that described in Nahum 2–3.

TO THINK ABOUT AND DISCUSS

1. The Assyrian empire was extremely militaristic, committed great atrocities and was characterized by extreme cruelty. However, like the German Third Reich, it fell with a mighty crash and was completely obliterated. Why was the judgement on Assyria so appropriate?

2. Nineveh set itself up against God's authority (2:15). Why is there ultimately no security in self-security?

3. How would you go about giving advice to a church leader who is showing signs of forgetting that he is a servant of Christ and his people?

8 Danger at home

(3:1–4)

'Woe,' thunders out the voice of the prophet, yet this is but a pale reflection of the anger that lies in the heart of the Almighty One. He is furious with all the nations that surround Judah—Philistia, Moab and Ammon—but most of all his anger is directed towards Nineveh, the city which carried out such cruelty and aggression against huge numbers of people (2:4–15).

No doubt the citizens of Judah were heartened to learn that their God was outraged with these wicked cities, just as an older brother might secretly snigger when a younger one is chastised by his parent. They had probably been gloating because God was berating these heathen cities and were probably glad when 'woe' was pronounced against 'the city of oppressors, rebellious and defiled' (3:1). However, on this occasion, God was not speaking about a range of places; rather his anger was directed against a specific city.

We can imagine the people of Jerusalem nodding their heads in mock disapproval when they heard about this city that 'obeys no one' and 'accepts no correction' (v. 2). It is likely that they assumed the prophet was still referring to the chief city of Assyria. Yet they would have begun to worry when they learned that this city '[did] not trust in the LORD'. Why did the prophet talk about this city not trusting 'the LORD'? That was the word that referred to the one true and living God; certainly 'the LORD' was not the god of Assyria.

So we can imagine the horror that would gradually have dawned upon them as they realized that God was actually speaking about them and their own beloved city of Jerusalem! This is what puzzled them: they knew they were God's chosen people, so how could he speak words of judgement upon them?

God's description of Jerusalem

Let us see how God viewed Jerusalem. Zephaniah, passing on the Lord's message, called it 'the city of oppressors'. Their forefathers had known what it was like to be oppressed by Egyptian slavery because the pain of those events would have been passed on to all the people from their childhood onwards; they understood what it was like to be badly treated. In Jeremiah's prophecy, the king of Judah was required to 'Rescue from the hand of his oppressor the one who has been robbed' (Jer. 22:3), yet here we see that Jerusalem is now called, in the English version of Calvin's translation, 'the city which is an oppressor'![1]

In what way could Jerusalem be called 'the city of oppressors'? Zephaniah went on to explain. It was because 'her rulers are evening wolves, who leave nothing for the morning. Her prophets are arrogant [and] treacherous ... Her priests profane the sanctuary and do violence to the law [of the Lord]' (v. 3). The general population knew about these injustices yet raised no objection.

Her officials and rulers

My wife and I visited a number of South African game parks early in 2007. There we learned a great deal about the various wild animals and about how much information can be gleaned from examining what these beasts leave behind (this is not a nice subject for the dinner table!). Rhinoceros dung has its own story to tell, but so too do the hard, white droppings of the hyena. I was reminded of this when I read about the 'evening wolves, who leave nothing for the morning' (v. 3). After the big cats have had their fill of any kill in the bush, the hyenas eat up everything that is left— including the bones.

The people of Jerusalem would have known about such animals. When God called the officials of the city 'evening wolves', he meant that they devoured everything for themselves and left nothing at all for those who were badly off. Amos 5:12 tells us that the poor of Israel were deprived of justice (because they could not afford to bribe the judges). It was the same in Jerusalem. Quite often, justice was only for those who could afford to pay money to the judges to find in their favour.

The people were also kept in order by the city officials,

who exercised their power over them by roaring like lions (v. 3). They were like the 'loan sharks' of our day, who lend money to those in financial need and then force them to sign a document which means they have to pay back many, many times the original loan if they default on the repayments. Some people have even had to sell their houses to pay their debts when they have only borrowed a few thousand pounds.

Jerusalem is also called 'rebellious and defiled'. She was a city that 'obeys no one, [and] accepts no correction'. In other words, the citizens were self-sufficient; they believed they knew better than anyone else. They did not 'trust in the LORD' because they felt they had no need of his presence; neither did they 'draw near to [their] God'.

> Because they forgot that they had been favoured with great privileges by the Lord, their guilt was even greater than that of their wicked neighbours.

They were behaving just like the people of the heathen cities that surrounded them. Because they forgot that they had been favoured with great privileges by the Lord, their guilt was even greater than that of their wicked neighbours. The assurance of God's presence had lulled them into a false sense of security so that they felt they could behave as they wished, just like the heathen around them. Their worship lacked sincerity, too. The phrase 'draw near to … God' was a description of true worship, yet the people had merely been going through the motions when they went up to the temple and engaged in their daily prayers. It was just ritual, devoid of all spiritual meaning.

So many churches today have imbibed a great many of the characteristics of the world around them. While the idea of 'seeker-friendly' services may be laudable as an attempt to draw people into the church, some churches have now even removed copies of the Bible from the seats on the grounds that 'people don't read these days'. Also, their music mimics that of the dance hall. This is nothing new. Many years ago, after attending a certain church, an unsaved friend of mine told me that she would not go again. She said, 'If I wanted to go to a disco I'd go to a dance hall, not a church.'

Having dealt in general with the people of Jerusalem and the city officials, Zephaniah now turns to the religious leaders. Moses, under the Lord's instructions, had given them a system of religious leaders: prophets to urge them to keep God's law and priests to preside over their worship. God tells the people that these will not escape God's condemnation either. The message that the Lord has for these leaders is as severe as that for the rulers.

Her religious leaders

Zephaniah, who as a prophet himself knew about the responsibilities of the task, says of Jerusalem, 'Her prophets are arrogant; they are treacherous men' (v. 4). It is a solemn responsibility to be a religious leader among the people of God. Just as these prophets of Zephaniah's day were 'arrogant' and 'treacherous men', so sometimes today there are people on the leadership teams of churches who behave like this. They have been appointed, not because they have the spiritual qualifications laid down in God's Word, but because they are popular individuals, or have the necessary technical skills, or the ability to lead people in the way the pastors desire.

The prophets may have been learned professional men, like Isaiah, or they may have been humble country folk, like Amos, but all of them had one thing in common—they had received a special call from God and they knew that their task was to pass on God's words to the people without deviating from them or adding to them.

So why did God call these prophets 'arrogant' and 'treacherous'? It was because they were anxious to bring their own ideas and views before the people and present them as God's words. It is egotistical in the extreme to stand up before the people of God and say, 'This is what the Lord says' if the message has not come from God. The way in which we can test whether such people are false prophets is by measuring their words against those of Holy Scripture. Recently I heard a preacher say, 'We must not try to bring our words up to the level of the Bible, nor must we seek to drag the Bible down to our human understanding.'

The prophets of whom Zephaniah spoke were those who loved to be noticed. Yet they were not merely proud and boastful: they were treacherous, too. They sought their own advantage and did so at the expense of the ordinary people. They were dangerous, because they deceived the people who had been taught to look up to them, and they did not speak the truth. Jeremiah 28:1–17 and 29:21–23 tells us about the folly of listening to prophets who tell lies.

Next, Zephaniah turns to the priests. Their main

responsibility was to represent men before God. Yet these priests, by their actions and attitude, had profaned the sanctuary. Their sacrifices and religious ceremonial had been carried out merely as a matter of routine instead of with holy reverence. Throughout the Old Testament, God emphasizes that he desires obedience to his law rather than sacrifice (see 'For further study' question 2 below).

Sadly, it is religious leaders who have brought the cause of Christ into disrepute today. As long ago as 1977, Dr J. Vernon McGee wrote of such people, 'They have caused the world outside to lose respect for that which was sacred.' He continued, 'I do not think that the church deserves the respect of the outside world when we cannot and do not present to them a church that is holy and that is living for God.'[2]

Not only did these priests fail to carry out their religious ritual with sanctity, but they also neglected their other responsibilities—to teach the people how to observe the law of the Lord. Jeremiah tells us how some of the priests behaved, making God's house 'a den of robbers' (Jer. 7:8–11) because they were manipulating the law of God chiefly to fill their own pockets.[3]

Being in leadership of a church and congregation is a very responsible thing. Church leaders can be a great blessing to God's people or they can be a disaster, as these were in Jerusalem in the days of Zephaniah. All church leaders and individual Christian believers should make sure that they are always living out the teaching of God's Word, otherwise they will be in danger of deceiving the people of God.

For further study ▶

FOR FURTHER STUDY

1. Study the character and work of the following Old Testament prophets: Moses (Deut. 18:15–22), Elijah (1 Kings 17:1; 18:15), Isaiah (Isa. 6:1–13, plus the rest of his prophecy), Amos (Amos 7:14–15), Jonah (Jonah 1:1; 3:1) and Haggai (Hag. 1:1–10).
2. Study the following Old Testament passages that speak of God's desire for obedience rather than sacrifice: 1 Samuel 15:22; Psalm 40:6–8; 51:16; Proverbs 21:3; Isaiah 1:11–15; Jeremiah 7:22; Hosea 6:6; Amos 5:25; Micah 6:6–8.
3. Examine the qualities required for leadership in God's church: 1 Timothy 3:1–13; Titus 1:5–9; Acts 20:28. Do you, or your church leaders, measure up to these high demands?

TO THINK ABOUT AND DISCUSS

1. 'All that is necessary for the triumph of evil is that good men do nothing' (Edmund Burke). How true is this in the church?
2. '[They] made me take care of the vineyards; my own vineyard I have neglected' (Song of Songs 1:6). What value do you place on your home and family? Share some of your shortcomings. How do you plan to ensure that your home and family are protected not only physically but also spiritually?
3. Read the solemn warning at the end of the Bible in Revelation 22:18–19. Are you guilty of taking away from the words of the Bible (e.g. by seeking to minimize their importance) or adding to them (e.g. by bringing in other values which are not consistent with the teaching of God's Word)? If so, what should you do about it?
4. In Galatians 6:10, Paul urges the believers there to 'Do good to all people, especially to those who belong to the family of believers.' Discuss how you and your church pastoral team are caring for all the members of your church, especially those who are particularly needy.

9 God's amazing grace

(3:5–8)

So far in Zephaniah's prophecy there has been an almost unending catalogue of gloom, but now, for the first time, we spot a glimmer of light. This is revealed when the character of the city of Jerusalem, in all its wickedness, is vividly contrasted with the holiness of God.

One of the best-known verses in Habakkuk's little prophecy makes a very serious point about the holy character of God: 'Your eyes are too pure to look on evil; you cannot tolerate wrong' (Hab. 1:13). Therefore, because much evil had been done in Jerusalem, we would expect the Lord to act quickly to remove the city from his presence. Remarkably, instead of doing this, the Lord gently reminds his people of his gracious presence with them, even though they have been so rebellious. Perhaps Zephaniah himself is perplexed as he passes on this statement: 'The LORD within her is righteous; he does no wrong' (3:5a). It is the phrase 'within her' that is so surprising. Their powerful God is not hovering on the outside of the city waiting to see whether the people will amend their ways; no, he is right there in the midst, just as he has always been with his people. Despite their terrible disobedience, God tells Jerusalem that he has not deserted it.

How gracious is the Lord to us! He does not act like some petulant employer, parent or friend who threatens to have nothing more to do with us because we have displeased him by our conduct or failure to act. Instead, just as the Lord informed Jerusalem that he was within her and promised to remain there, so the Lord has promised to be with his chosen ones today (see Deut. 31:6; Heb. 13:6).

> We can learn two important lessons from this. Firstly, regardless of our conduct, God does not change his character ... Secondly, he is, always has been and will continue to be 'righteous'.

We can learn two important lessons from this. Firstly, regardless of our conduct, God does not change his character; he may change his actions, but not his nature. Secondly, he is, always has been and will continue to be 'righteous'. However much he is provoked, he will do no wrong.

Yet the Lord is not idle; he is active and continues to dispense justice to the city (because he behaves in right ways—in other words, he is righteous, v. 5). The few

Judeans who remained faithful to the Lord would have known the truth of this. Commentary on the words of verse 5 has been included in a good number of Christian hymns and songs, such as:

> Great is thy faithfulness!
> Great is thy faithfulness!
> Morning by morning new mercies I see.
> All I have needed thy hand hath provided;
> Great is thy faithfulness, Lord, unto me![1]

And:

> New every morning is the love
> Our wakening and uprising prove;
> Through sleep and darkness safely brought,
> Restored to life and power and thought.[2]

Justice is the keynote of all God's activity. He never fails to dispense his blessings, even to those who do not deserve them. In hot countries, important business was conducted in the early morning before the rays of the sun blazed down. By saying 'Morning by morning he dispenses his justice', the prophet may be referring to those judges who were still faithful to the Lord and who sat at the city gates to mediate justice for the people. They had been consistent in their fairness, doing this work every morning. Certainly verse 5 speaks of God's common grace, which he pours out on all people. The sunshine and the rain fall equally upon those who are righteous and those who are wicked (see Matt. 5:45).

With this assurance of the Lord's presence and his continual grace 'every new day', one would expect that the people would be so overwhelmed with gratitude that they would hurry to make amends for their bad behaviour—but no. They remained unrighteous and continued to have no shame about their conduct.

Unsaved people who will not be deterred from selfishness and evil actions continue to live with the thought that they are immune from God's displeasure. Some are content merely to know that the Lord is around and that he is a righteous God. Such people would not call themselves atheists or agnostics, yet they have no desire to be intimate with God or to take too much trouble to obey his laws. They claim to be Christian people, and so they believe that everything will turn out all right in the end. They think they will 'muddle through' until they get old, and then perhaps they will turn to 'religion'. How foolish such people are! They forget that it is not only the old who die. Disease, accident and warfare are no respecters of age. Death will strike all people down, whether they have made appropriate preparations to meet their God or not. In these days in the West, when far more people are comparatively well off, such people continue to 'build bigger barns', not realizing that the Lord may demand their life at any time (see Luke 12:16–20).

The warnings given to Jerusalem (vv. 6–8)

The people of Judah only had to look around them to see that the Lord had already been active in cutting off nations; so many of them had been destroyed. Even those cities which had apparently secure strongholds had been destroyed

(v. 6—Zephaniah may have been referring to the corner towers of the cities), and their once-busy streets had been left devoid of people. Who had done this? Zephaniah tells the Judeans that it is the Lord: 'I have cut off nations … I have left their streets deserted.' The evidence is there before the eyes of all who pass by, especially these citizens of Jerusalem. If they take the trouble to look, they will observe that no one is left in those cities that God has demolished.

They will then know that God is serious when he says that he will punish those who persist in their wickedness. In verse 7, the Lord reasons like a human being: 'After you have seen what I have done to those wicked, unrepentant cities around you, surely you will fear me and accept correction!' He says to them, 'If you repent (that is, accept correction and all that goes with it), then your dwelling will not be cut off, nor will all my punishments come upon you.'

Anyone with a modicum of sense would be able to see the wisdom in the Lord's argument and would eagerly rush to the Lord with gratitude and a sincere desire to turn from wicked ways and return to God's paths. But these people, God's own chosen people, although eager, were not willing to do the right thing. Instead, they acted 'corruptly in all they did'. They did not even turn aside from some of their wickedness; rather they continued to act corruptly in *everything* they did.

'There are none so blind as those who will not see' is an old saying that is still true today. Some people do not want to be confused by facts. Nothing will bring them to their senses, and they persist in their foolish ways. They behave like those of Peter's day and say, 'Where is this "coming" he promised?

Ever since our fathers died, everything goes on as it has since the beginning of creation' (2 Peter 3:4). Those people of New Testament times conveniently forgot that things have not gone on just as they had since the beginning of creation. Peter forcefully reminded them that they were blind and deaf; the Flood came and destroyed all living things that were not inside the safety of the ark. Those people of earlier times chose to ignore the judgement that God had brought upon the cities that surrounded them.

Sadly, so many people carry on today without giving any heed to God's laws or his commands. Like these Judeans of old, they believe that 'The LORD will do nothing, either good or bad' (see 1:12). Yet the evidence is all around us that we will not live for ever. As morals decay and crime and violence are on the increase in our day, the warning is clear that God will bring judgement upon unrepentant sinners. The call goes out for sinners to turn back again to the Lord and find rest in him, which is the only place where true and lasting peace can be found.

This section ends with God's announcement of a final and complete judgement upon sin and sinners (v. 8). The Lord will stand up to testify; he will assemble all the nations and their kingdoms so that he may pour out his wrath on them. 'The whole world will be consumed by the fire of [his] jealous anger.'

For many, this will be the end, but the final verses of Zephaniah's prophecy tell us of God's fire that purifies as well as consumes (v. 9).

FOR FURTHER STUDY

1. Study what the Bible says about those who persist in wickedness: 1 Samuel 12:24–25; Isaiah 26:10; 59:7.

2. Why do some Christian people refuse to take heed of God's pleadings and his warnings? (See Luke 19:41–44; Luke 13:34–35; Lev. 26:31–32; Ps. 69:25; Micah 3:9–12.)

3. What use can we make of God's many calls to return to him? (See Isa. 55:1,6; Amos 5:4–5; Matt. 11:28; John 7:37.)

TO THINK ABOUT AND DISCUSS

1. The civil, judicial and religious leaders of Jerusalem were specially selected for judgement (3:3–4). Why were they held accountable for 'the city of oppressors'? Will church leaders today be held similarly responsible?

2. Why do people fail to take notice of the warnings of God's judgement upon today's society?

10 The blessings of 'that day'

(3:9–13)

We are brought up with a start when we read the first word in verse 9: 'then'. The Lord is talking about what he will do on 'that day' (or at 'that time')—this is the same day that he has referred to many times in this prophecy (see 1:7–10,12,14–16,18; 2:2–3; 3:8,11,16,19–20). With most of the previous uses of 'the day of the LORD', we have seen that it will bring about a great calamity on the whole earth and evil will be destroyed.

Often, mention of this day is accompanied by the Lord saying, 'I will ...' We sometimes say that we will do a certain thing at a specific time, but events press in and prevent us from doing what we promise. However, unlike us, the Lord is never surprised by events because he knows all things and acts to carry out his will.

Jerusalem, sadly, was filled with disobedient people whose worship was but empty ritual and whose morals were faulty. Because she would not heed God's gracious calls to repentance, he promised that one day he would 'cut off' her dwelling (v. 7). This occasion would result in the summing up of all their sins and failures and would cause him to turn away from them. It would be the end for this people, even though they claimed to be the people of God; he was going to pour out the fire of his jealous anger upon them (v. 8).

Yet, in the midst of all this talk of destruction, we read these wonderful words: 'Then will I purify the lips of the peoples, that all of them may call on the name of the LORD and serve him shoulder to shoulder.' Evil actions start in the mind, and one of the ways in which they display themselves is in harsh words. James gives us a terrifying description of the damage that can be caused by that small part of our bodies, the tongue. He tells us, 'The tongue ... is a fire, a world of evil among the parts of the body. It corrupts the whole person, sets the whole course of his life on fire, and is itself set on fire by hell' (James 3:6). The Puritan Thomas Brooks put it like this: 'Of all the members in the body, there is none so serviceable to Satan as the tongue'; and Morris Gliber wrote, 'The jawbone of an ass was a killer in Samson's time. It still is.'[1] However, 'that day' would not only usher in destruction on those who were disobedient, but it would also bring salvation on 'the remnant of Israel' (v. 13). This deliverance would not be something that the people could do for themselves; God says, '*I* will purify.' In the last twelve verses of Zephaniah, we read details of the activity of the Lord that would bring blessing on the people, usually indicated by the phrase 'I will ...' (or '... will I ...').

No one can call upon the name of the Lord with unclean lips. The only exception is that of a repentant sinner who is crying to the Lord for mercy. When the Lord called Isaiah, he demurred, saying, 'I am a man of unclean lips, and I live among a people of unclean lips' (Isa. 6:5); when Simon Peter's eyes were opened for the first time to see the Lord Jesus Christ for who he really was, he called out, 'Go away from me, Lord; I am a sinful man!' (Luke 5:8). Neither Isaiah nor Peter really wanted the Lord to leave them; they both just felt so unworthy of the task to which they were being called that they could not understand why the Lord would want to use them in his service. The people of Jerusalem in Zephaniah's time, however, had no concept of the utter defilement of their hearts (3:1). Even so, the Lord promised that some of them would be purified and go forward to serve him 'shoulder to shoulder' with their fellows who had also been redeemed from their sin. These were the members of the remnant to which Zephaniah and other prophets made many references.

This mention of working 'shoulder to shoulder' speaks of the unity of God's people. Disunity in the church causes enormous trouble and brings dishonour on God's name. Jesus prayed that his people might be one (John 17:21), and this is the desire of all true leaders of God's people today. Being united does not necessarily mean that everyone agrees on every single issue or takes the same stance in every discussion, but it does mean that everyone's aim is the same: to bring glory to God and further his gospel message. When writing to his beloved Philippian church, Paul wrote that he prayed that they would 'stand firm in one spirit, contending as one man for the faith of the gospel' (Phil. 1:27).

However, this unity would not be merely a unity of those who lived in Jerusalem and were true to the Lord; it also applied to those faithful ones who were scattered afar 'from beyond the rivers of Cush' (v. 10). This refers to Ethiopia and the regions near the source of the river Nile. This whole area of Africa would have been considered extremely remote by the Judeans, yet God promised that those scattered people who knew him and worshipped him would bring offerings to the Lord.

In other words, God was graciously telling the faithful ones in Jerusalem that they were not on their own. There were many others who had not bowed the knee to foreign gods (who are no gods at all). These words

> Even though the enemy of souls, the devil, may seem to be winning in his battle to thwart God's purposes, he will not succeed.

bring great comfort to suffering Christians today. Even though the enemy of souls, the devil, may seem to be winning in his battle to thwart God's purposes, he will not succeed. None of us stands alone in concern to maintain God's honour. Not only can we be assured that our God is with us, but we are also told here, and elsewhere, that there are countless numbers of believers spread all around the globe who are standing with us as we worship the Lord in the beauty of holiness. Anthony Selvaggio puts it like this: 'In the new day described by Zephaniah, God's people will include all nations; they will be humble and they will be holy.'[2]

Through the gospel proclamation, many from 'every tribe and language and people and nation' have been made into a people for God and his glory (Rev. 5:9). By the cross, the division between Jew and Gentile has been broken down, like the removal of a wall of hostility, through the Lord Jesus Christ's death; and now repentant sinners can find peace and joy through his blood (see Eph. 2:14–17).

Blessings for Jerusalem itself

Although God had described the city as 'rebellious and defiled' (v. 1), when the day of the Lord dawned she would be transformed so that she would experience no shame for all the wrong she had done to her God. Here again we see gracious blessings of the good news of salvation. What is one of the first things felt by a sinner who has been convicted of his or her sin under the preaching of the gospel? It is an overwhelming sense of disobedience and sinfulness. Conviction of sin is something that is, sadly, rarely mentioned in testimonies of newly converted people; naturally they want to tell us of the joy and excitement they experienced when they became Christians, but conversion experience seldom starts with happiness.

In Zephaniah 3:11, the prophet alludes to the sin of the people by telling them that, on that day, they will not be put to shame even though they will feel a deep sense of their sinful past. Why is this? It is because all of their sins (which are numerous) will be washed away and they will be cleansed. They will no longer feel the burden of the guilt of their wrongdoing. This is what a saved sinner experiences after having turned from sin and come to Christ in simple, humble belief, trusting in his blood and righteousness. Paul tells us that 'there is now no condemnation for those who are in Christ Jesus' (Rom. 8:1).

The gospel message, like the events depicted here in Zephaniah 3:11, will bring a division between the people of God and those who desire to continue in their sinful ways. This division will be brought about by the Lord himself. He will 'remove from this city those who rejoice in their pride'. God cannot tolerate pride in his people. Our only boast should be in the Lord (see 1 Cor. 1:31).

When God has removed from the city those who 'rejoice in their pride', the purified ones who are left within the city will be 'meek and humble' and will 'trust in the name of the LORD'. They will have no hope in themselves or in their abilities; their reliance will be in the Lord alone, because he has purified their lips and their hearts and has redeemed them. They will have a brand new attitude and purpose. They will be like their Lord: verse 5 tells us that he does no wrong, and now we are told that 'The remnant of Israel will do no wrong' (v. 13). This is because they will then have a new heart and a new spirit. No longer will their life be dominated by selfishness. Rebellion and pride will also have been removed, because they have been 'born again'; henceforth they will live a new life (see Rom. 6:5–7).

Truth will now characterize their speech. Unlike the majority of prophets who resided in Jerusalem (who were 'treacherous'—v. 4), these 'newborn' people will always speak the truth, 'nor will deceit be found in their mouths'.

Their transformation will be like that of Jacob to Israel when he changed from being a deceiver into a prince of God.

From the bustling city which has been intent upon selfish aggrandizement, the scene becomes pastoral, describing a place where they will 'eat and lie down and no one will make them afraid'. No longer will their shepherds (the false priests and prophets of v. 4) 'feed themselves' (Ezek. 34:10), but the Good Shepherd will 'tend them in a good pasture, and the mountain heights of Israel will be their grazing land. There they will lie down in good grazing land, and there they will feed in a rich pasture on the mountains of Israel' (Ezek. 34:14).

Throughout both of the Old and New Testaments, we have many allusions to the people of God as his flock. Micah changes the figure slightly but keeps the pastoral scene when he says, 'Every man will sit under his own vine and under his own fig tree [which will give both fruit and shade], and no one will make them afraid', because they experience the security of God's presence (Micah 4:4).

FOR FURTHER STUDY

1. What are the dangers of an unruly tongue? (See Matt. 12:36; Eph. 4:29–31; 5:4; Col. 3:8.)

2. Carefully read though the last twelve verses of Zephaniah. Make a list of all the things God promises to do to bring blessing on his people.

3. Study the geographical extent of God's people from the following Scriptures: 1 Kings 8:41–43; Psalm 22:27; 102:22; Isaiah 2:2–4; 18:7; 19:18–25; 56:1–7; Malachi 1:11; Acts 8:26–39.

TO THINK ABOUT AND DISCUSS

1. Read through this small prophecy of Zephaniah again and note the times that the Lord says he will do something. What can we learn from God's actions, and how should we alter our behaviour to conform to the teaching in this prophecy?

2. Paul tells us, 'Do not let any unwholesome talk come out of your mouths, but only what is helpful for building others up according to their needs' (Eph. 4:29). What practical steps can we take to curb our tongues?

3. No one likes a proud person. How can we live our lives with more humility? How can we avoid pride?

4. Discuss the security and peace that God's people experience when he is their Shepherd (see Ps. 23; 100; John 10:11–17; Heb. 13:20; 1 Peter 5:4).

11 Rejoicing at the King's presence

(3:14–17)

As we approach the last seven verses of
Zephaniah, we find a totally different
atmosphere from that which pervaded the
earlier part of this prophecy. Zephaniah is now
full of praise and thanksgiving because of the
news that God will deliver and comfort his
repentant people.

When this salvation arrives, the citizens of
Jerusalem will be so full of joy that they will
'sing', 'shout aloud', 'be glad' and 'rejoice'
(v. 14). However, at the time that Zephaniah
is telling them about this, he is not referring to the Jerusalem
of his day: he is looking way into the future, yet speaking as
though that coming glorious day has already arrived.

The reason for such excitement will be because all God's
faithful people will know in those coming days that the Lord

has taken away all threat of punishment from them. Despite the former bad behaviour of the citizens of Jerusalem, he promises to dwell among them. This will not be just for a while: he will dwell with them for ever (v. 15).

Zephaniah was not the only prophet to speak in these terms; Zechariah also told of the joy that will be experienced when the King comes. He cried out, 'Rejoice greatly, O Daughter of Zion! Shout, Daughter of Jerusalem! See, your king comes to you, righteous and having salvation, gentle and riding on a donkey, on a colt, the foal of a donkey' (Zech. 9:9).

No doubt the piling up of all Zephaniah's tremendous words of adulation would have appeared to be grossly 'over the top', because those who were faithful among the people were very conscious of their wrongdoing and knew that it would bring God's judgement upon the city.

Whenever a believer becomes aware of God's offer of forgiveness, he or she feels unworthy. Isaiah was not filled with excitement and joy when he saw the Lord seated on a throne, high and exalted. No, he cried, 'Woe to me! ... I am ruined! For I am a man of unclean lips ... and my eyes have seen the King, the LORD Almighty' (Isa. 6:1,5). In the same way, these Judeans would feel ashamed of their sinfulness, but that did not alter the fact that they were going to be forgiven and set free.

Throughout the history of God's people, we see that the joy of God's salvation has not been expressed in a frivolous exhilaration. The experience of forgiven sins is a 'deep-down' joy which often expresses itself in quiet, rapturous delight. Sadly, during 'the time of worship' (which some people call 'singing'), the scene can be similar to that at a pop concert attended by youngsters when a well-known group is performing.

Gary Gilley believes that preachers in some churches are ignoring the solemn fact that God 'will punish those who do not know God and do not obey the gospel of our Lord Jesus' (2 Thes. 1:8). These preachers are wary of sermons that might deter people from becoming Christians. Instead, they preach that 'Christ will meet all of their felt needs and that will lead to personal fulfilment'. The members of their congregations are being 'asked to trust in Christ, the great "Needs-Meeter", who will end [their] search for a life of happiness and fulfilment'.[1]

Zephaniah may have been referring to that day, seventy years or so in the future, when Jewish people were finally set free from the Babylonian captivity. As they journeyed back to Jerusalem, they would have had a certain measure of contentment—even happiness—to be going home, yet they would also have been very weary from the effects of the long and tedious journey. Furthermore, we know from the events recorded in the books of Nehemiah and Haggai that the rebuilding of the walls of Jerusalem and the temple would mean much hard work and disappointment for them all. As great as the rejoicing would be when they returned from Babylon, it is obvious that the words of verses 14–17 referred to an event even greater than the restoration of Judah from captivity.

The quotation above from Zechariah reinforces this view, because Matthew makes it clear that Zechariah was referring to the time when the Lord Jesus Christ rode into

Jerusalem on 'a colt, the foal of a donkey' (Matt. 21:5). However, even that day was not the major fulfilment of Zechariah's prophecy, because we know that those cries of 'Hosanna to the Son of David!' (Matt. 21:9) were transformed only a few days later into yells of 'Crucify him!' (Matt. 27:22). So, the events referred to in Zephaniah 3:14–17 are surely pointing to a day which has still not yet arrived. They refer to that glorious coming day, when 'the earth will be filled with the knowledge of the glory of the LORD, as the waters cover the sea' (Hab. 2:14). That will be a day when there will be 'no more death or mourning or crying or pain' (Rev. 21:4)—a day when each redeemed soul is 'a secured soul, a safe and a happy soul'.[2]

Three reasons for rejoicing

The first cause for rejoicing given by Zephaniah is this wonderful statement: 'The LORD has taken away your punishment.' I sometimes try to imagine what it must feel like to be standing in the dock in a court of law and learn that I have been found guilty of a crime so heinous that the judge has to put on his black cap and say, 'It is the sentence of this court that you should be taken from this place to the prison whence you came, and from there to a place of execution where you shall be hanged by the neck until you are dead. May God have mercy on your soul.'

Surely the knowledge that I have carried out such a terrible crime that my life is going to be taken from me would be a terrifying thing. Would I want the execution to take place quickly so I did not have too much time to think about it, or would I long for it to be delayed as much as possible with the hope of a reprieve? Such a condemned man must be full of dread.

The people of Jerusalem who had been faithful to the Lord would have been similar. They would have known that their city was filled with oppression, rebellion and defilement (v. 1) and that therefore they were guilty with the rest of the people. They would have dreaded the punishment that would surely come upon them. They had already seen the Lord's action in bringing the dreaded Assyrian invaders down upon their northern neighbour, Israel, and they had surely heard about the vicious cruelty meted out to them. With those thoughts as their constant companions, we can imagine something of the glorious sound these wonderful words would have made: 'The LORD has taken away your punishment!'

> It is only as we appreciate the dreadfulness of our sin before the holiness of God that we can fully realize the blessedness of sins forgiven.

Sadly, we sometimes glibly recite, 'Forgive us our sins, as we forgive those who have sinned against us' (see Luke 11:4), but when prayed without feeling, those words do not convey to us the blessedness of sins forgiven. It is only as we appreciate the dreadfulness of our sin before the holiness of God that we can fully realize the blessedness of sins forgiven. It is worth noting that both the New King James Version and the English Standard Version render the word translated 'punishment' in the New International Version in the plural; the sins of Jerusalem were therefore very great.

My wife and I have recently started to attend a good Anglican church. When it comes to the style of the service, we are finding very few things to be different from our previous nonconformist churches. However, what is striking is this: at most services we are asked to prepare ourselves for a time of confession. This is no bland 'vain repetition' of well-known words; we are urged to be quiet before the Lord and privately confess our sins to him. Only after that do we say these, or similar, words: 'Most merciful God, Father of our Lord Jesus Christ, we confess that we have sinned in thought, word and deed. We have not loved you with our whole heart. We have not loved our neighbours as ourselves. In your mercy forgive what we have been, help us to amend what we are, and direct what we shall be; that we may do justly, love mercy, and walk humbly with you, our God. Amen.'[3]

Zephaniah's second cause for rejoicing is because the Lord 'has turned back [their] enemy'. I was five years old and living in Kent when Nazi Germany swiftly invaded the Low Countries and then France so that Hitler could stand and view the white cliffs of Dover through a powerful telescope. I remember large trenches being dug in the fields near my home to make it difficult for enemy tanks to cross into the town. Also, every straight piece of road had round or conical-shaped pieces of concrete placed near it; these were supposed to be rolled into the middle of the road to prevent enemy aircraft landing on it. In those days, the whole country was preparing for invasion, and many prayers were said for the safety of our land and its people. When our troops were captured or driven into the sea, the Lord provided a miracle and the English Channel was the calmest it had been for some while. This allowed some 338,226 of our troops to escape from Dunkirk and the surrounding areas. Christian people hailed this as the hand of God working to protect Britain from invasion by the enemies of civilization.

The armies of Assyria had come very near to Jerusalem, but God had turned them back. Later, when the Babylonians arrived in 586 BC, they took away the best among the Judeans; but even though this was going to happen in the future, Zephaniah wanted the people to know that their God was still in charge. Then, throughout their long years in captivity, they had this assurance that it would not last for ever: the Babylonians would eventually be overthrown. That was going to be an illustration of that ultimate victory granted to the Lord and his people. His promise in Deuteronomy 28:7 will always remain true: 'The LORD will grant that the enemies who rise up against you will be defeated before you.'

In order to sustain them when that time arrived, a third blessing was given: 'The LORD, the King of Israel, is with you.' These words must have thrilled them as they heard the prophet speak. The wonderful thing was that they were not just going to be visited by a dignitary: the King himself was coming to them, sinful though they were. That King is the one who is the only sovereign Ruler of the world, but he is not so exalted that he shows no care for others. The situation is quite the opposite: this almighty King has a special love and care for his own people. This was the glorious news. The King had not only taken away the punishment due to his faithful people in Jerusalem, but he had also turned away their enemies and promised to come and be with them for ever. This would ensure that they would never again 'fear any harm'.

This King, the Lord Jesus Christ, came to this earth in the days of the Romans, and he offered up his life on the cross as a ransom to pay the price for the sin of his wayward people. But this same King is going to return one day in the future, and then he will be with his people for ever. That is the long-term view of these events. The Lord's redeemed people are conscious of the Lord's presence with them every day, but this glorious King will return one day and rule supreme over mankind. On that great day there will be great rejoicing and gladness of heart.

God's people in Jerusalem would no longer find that they were not able to stretch out hands that had hung limply until that time. Formerly they had been so demoralized by the state of the city and its people that those hands which they used to do their work had hung forlornly at their sides. Now those same hands (that is, the people themselves) would be strengthened and put back to the work of praising the Lord (see Heb. 12:12).

As they listened to the words of Zephaniah, it would have gradually begun to dawn on the faithful ones of Jerusalem that they, who had been so useless to God and his work, were now being put to work again to bring praise and glory to his name. Just as the apostle Peter could hardly believe that he was being called back into the Lord's service after his disgraceful behaviour at the trial of Jesus (see Mark 14:66–72 and John 21:15–17), so it would have dawned upon the Judeans that the Lord had not only forgiven them, but he also actually took delight in them (v. 17).

Here we find something that is very surprising. God's

redeemed people would be filled with love and gratitude at the pouring out of his goodness and grace. They knew that those who do not 'walk in the counsel of the wicked' take 'delight ... in the law of the LORD' (Ps. 1:1–2) and that this God was their joy and delight (Ps. 43:4), but now they would be overwhelmed with the knowledge that the Lord would 'take great delight' in them (v. 17). How can such a holy God take delight in sinful people? It is because of his very nature and character: he is a God of mercy (Micah 7:18), and he takes delight in those whom he has redeemed from the slavery of sin (Deut. 30:9).

Those who had been so unsettled and disquieted by the sin and degradation of their surroundings would be swamped by the love of the King, and this King would even rejoice over his people with singing. Today, his people respond by singing songs such as this:

My Lord, what love is this
That pays so dearly,
That I, the guilty one,
May go free!

Amazing love! O what sacrifice,
The Son of God giv'n for me!
My debt he pays, and my death he dies
That I might live, that I might live.[4]

How great is our God that, when he sees us redeemed and made pure by the cleansing of Christ's precious blood, he will rejoice over us with singing!

1. Study the names given to God's people in verse 14. Read the following verses and note how these descriptions could apply to Christians today: 'Daughter of Zion' (Ps. 2:6; 48:2; Isa. 1:8); 'Israel' (Gen. 32:28); 'Daughter of Jerusalem' (Ps. 135:21; 137:5–6).

2. What does it mean to you to have the assurance that you will 'dwell in the house of the Lord forever' (Ps. 23:6)?

3. Study Peter's disgraceful behaviour and the Lord's forgiveness and renewed call back to service (see Mark 14:66–72; 16:7; John 21:15–19; Acts 2; 3:1–10; 8:14–25; 11:1–18). What can we learn from these Scriptures about repentance and forgiveness?

TO THINK ABOUT AND DISCUSS

1. What methods do you use to bring joy to your spirit when things are going very badly? Read Psalms 42–43 to see the psalmist's methods.

2. Can you think of a time when you or someone you know has been kept from a potentially disastrous situation? How can such experiences help us in our Christian walk?

3. How can we avoid situations when it feels as if the Lord has withdrawn his presence from us?

4. Study the parable of the Prodigal Son (Luke 15:11–32) from the point of view of the waiting father. Note the delight he shows at the wanderer's return. What can we learn from this parable about forgiving those who have wronged us?

12 God's time for restoration

(3:18–20)

After all the joy and excitement of the previous verses, this closing section of Zephaniah's prophecy seems almost like a disappointment— but it is not. The prophet is summarizing all that he has said and outlining some of those things that are still waiting to be fulfilled. The book ends with the same words that occur very near the beginning of the prophecy: 'says [or 'declares'] the LORD'.

People often complain, 'Why does God keep quiet when there is so much evil in the world?' Like a good parent, the Lord desires that his people learn to be patient and wait for him to act in his own good time and way. He will not be rushed into action. Ecclesiastes tells us, 'There is a time for everything, and a season for every activity under heaven' (Eccles. 3:1). God knows when the time is ripe for action, and, in the meantime, we must remember that he has not forsaken us; he is always watching over us.

In the last three verses of Zephaniah, God states, 'I will' seven times; this same verb, or a similar one, has already been used many times in the book. 'At that time' is also stated three times in the last two verses.

Previously these words had been used in the negative sense of ushering in God's judgement (see 1:2–4,8–9,12) but now we see them being used in a positive way. In 3:9 God says that he 'will' purify the lips of his faithful people, and in 3:11 he states that he 'will' remove the proud from the city. In the final three verses of the prophecy, God continues to tell his people what he 'will' do to help them.

A look into the fairly immediate future

The appointed feasts of Moses were not meant to be a burden to the people, but for some of those weary ones, no doubt, the ceremonies were becoming a trial. Similarly today, Christian people occasionally confess that attending worship has lost its freshness and excitement.

During the coming days of captivity in Babylon, God's people were going to be greatly distressed because the 'appointed feasts' would be difficult. Cut off from Jerusalem, they would have no access to the temple of the Lord. The taking away of those feasts was going to bring great sorrow for them.

While sitting by the waters of Babylon, they would weep every time they remembered Zion. They were going to ask, 'How can we sing the songs of the LORD while in a foreign land?' (Ps. 137). Yet, although they would no longer be able to go to the temple to worship God, they would still be able to look in its direction and remember with thanksgiving the joy of those feast days (just as Jonah did while he was inside the fish—Jonah 2:4–5). It was during this period in their history that synagogue worship was established as an alternative to travelling to Jerusalem. A synagogue was not a 'temple', 'church' or any holy building; rather it was merely a meeting place where the people could praise God and remember all his goodness. During the days of Jesus, synagogue worship was a regular feature of the people, and he went to the synagogue on Sabbath days. In Acts 16:13, while travelling in Philippi, Paul and Silas found a 'synagogue' by a riverside. It was not a building; it was a spot in the open air where Jewish women gathered (in that particular case it was not a genuine synagogue because it lacked any male attendees). For Christians today, 'the church' is not a building but the people of God gathered together. The word 'church' is never used of any building in the New Testament.

> ... 'the church' is not a building but the people of God gathered together. The word 'church' is never used of any building in the New Testament.

But here is the good news: although the righteous Jews were going to be sorrowful because of their removal from the temple, yet they were promised that there would be a day in the future when God would take away their sorrows. These appointed feasts would no longer be a burden because the Lord himself would be with them, in their midst. This would happen because the Lord had declared it.

Not only did God promise to restore to the faithful remnant the joy of true worship, but he also promised to remove all those who oppressed them now and in the future (v. 19; see also v. 15). Just as I, when a boy, used to tremble when my headmaster said with a menacing tone, 'I will deal with you later, boy', so the enemies of God's people would tremble to be dealt with by the supreme 'headteacher'. This One, who was willing and able to remove burdens and the reproach that lay upon God's people, would also rescue the lame (that is, God's people who had been incapacitated by their enemies) and gather those who had been scattered.

Zephaniah uses similar words in verse 19 to those used by Micah in Micah 4:6. Not only would God deliver them as individuals, 'he told them that he would restore them as a nation once again.'[1] At that time they were being threatened by the Assyrians; later, they would be separated from their beloved Jerusalem through their captivity in Babylon. However, just as the sovereign Lord 'tends his flock like a shepherd' and 'gathers the lambs in his arms' (Isa. 40:11), so the Lord would collect together the lame, despised and oppressed people of his flock and 'give them praise and honour in every land where they were put to shame.' 'The once-despised people of God now find themselves the objects of awe and respect from the surrounding nations.'[2]

At that time, the Lord will not only gather his people (and God's people delight to gather with the Lord Jesus Christ at the centre of their worship and social activities), he will also bring them home. The word 'home' conjures up in our minds a feeling of warmth, joy, welcome and a reminder of where we really belong. An old negro spiritual says,

This world is not my home, I'm just passing through.
My treasures are laid up somewhere beyond the blue.
The angels beckon me from Heaven's open door
and I can't feel at home in this world anymore.[3]

After seventeen months in the army in Kenya during the bitter and dangerous Mau Mau campaign, my heart sang as I hurried from the railway station in my home town with the eager anticipation of seeing my mum and dad. I was happy, because I was heading for home. It is true that Christians are 'at home' whenever they are with God's people, but they will be happier still when they 'go home' to their eternal rest after their days upon earth have come to an end.

God's people in Judah would not have to suffer continually. God would not only restore them to their land, but he would also 'restore their fortunes' to them; all the blessings of God's people would be theirs, and this would be done 'before [their] very eyes'. 'Before your very eyes' was a phrase used by a radio comedian of my youth. Presumably mimicking the tricks of conjurers, Arthur Askey used to promise that he would do things 'before your very eyes' in order to show that there was no sleight of hand.

But no such deceit will be used by the Lord. He will bring about his redemptive work before our very eyes. The final chapters of Revelation tell us some of the glories of that 'home' which awaits all of God's own blood-bought people:

'Now the dwelling of God is with men, and he will live with them. They will be his people, and God himself will be with them and be their God. He will wipe every tear from their eyes. There will be no more death or mourning or crying or pain, for the old order of things has passed away.'

He who was seated on the throne said, 'I am making everything new! ... To him who is thirsty I will give to drink without cost from the spring of the water of life. He who overcomes will inherit all this, and I will be his God and he will be my son' (Rev. 21:3–7).

Twice in these last few verses of Zephaniah we read these remarkable words: 'I will give them [or 'you'] praise and honour' (vv. 19–20). This is a remarkable statement, and we want to say, 'I don't deserve such acclaim.' Of course that is true: God's blood-bought people are going to receive much honour and praise, but none of it is because they merit it or have earned it in any way. It is purely by God's own pleasure and will that these blessings will be granted.

It is also a fulfilment of the promise made in Deuteronomy 26:19: 'He has declared that he will set you in praise, fame and honour high above all the nations he has made and that you will be a people holy to the LORD your God, as he promised' (see also Jer. 13:11). These feeble Jews (see Neh. 4:2) would be honoured and respected 'in every land where they were put to shame'.

God's people today are promised the same blessings. Though the church is bruised, battered and persecuted in some parts of the world today—and in many other places Christians are seen as a despised and worthless people—yet God's word is true and it will come to pass: one day, his people are going to 'receive honour and praise among all the peoples of the earth'.

For further study ▶

FOR FURTHER STUDY

1. What is the most important element in Christian worship? (See 1 Kings 8:57; Hag. 1:13; Matt. 18:20; 28:20; Acts 18:10.)

2. Why does Peter call the new heaven and earth 'the home of righteousness'? (See 2 Peter 3:13; Isa. 11:4–5; 45:8; Dan. 9:24.)

TO THINK ABOUT AND DISCUSS

1. What steps can you take to ensure that religious observance does not become a chore?

2. Can true worship of God be conducted in a building which has not been religiously consecrated for worship? Explain your answer.

For further reading

David W. Baker, *Nahum, Habakkuk and Zephaniah* (Tyndale Old Testament Commentaries) (Leicester: IVP, 1988).

John Calvin, *Commentaries on the Minor Prophets* (Grand Rapids, MI: Baker, n.d). (Other editions of Calvin's works are available.)

Gareth Crossley, *The Old Testament Explained and Applied* (Darlington: Evangelical Press, 2002).

F. Davidson (ed.), *The New Bible Commentary* (London: IVP, 1953).

Mariano DiGangi, *Twelve Prophetic Voices* (Wheaton, IL: Victor Books, 1985).

R. K. Harrison, *Introduction to the Old Testament* (London: Tyndale Press, 1970).

Robert Hawker, *Commentary on the Holy Bible* (London: Sherwood, Neeley and Jones, 1822).

Matthew Henry, *Commentary on the Whole Bible* (London: Marshall, Morgan and Scott, 1960). (There are various editions of this work, which was originally published in 1701.)

Theo Laetsch, *The Minor Prophets* (St Louis, MO: Concordia Publishing House, 1956).

J. Vernon McGee, *Commentary #31: Zephaniah and Haggai* (Pasadena, CA: Thru the Bible Books, 1979).

Anthony Selvaggio, *The Prophets Speak of Him* (Darlington: Evangelical Press, 2006).

Daniel Webber, *The Coming of the Warrior-King* (Darlington: Evangelical Press, 2004).

David Hewetson, *Zephaniah: Bible Probe* (Homebush West, NSW: Anzea Books, 1981).

Endnotes

Chapter 1

1 **David W. Baker,** *Nahum, Habakkuk and Zephaniah*, Tyndale Old Testament Commentaries (Leicester: IVP, 1988), p. 92.

2 **Daniel Webber,** *The Coming of the Warrior-King*, (Darlington: Evangelical Press, 2004), p. 47.

3 For a review of the Market-Driven Church movement, see **Gary Gilley,** *This Little Church Went to Market* (Darlington: Evangelical Press, 2005).

Chapter 2

1 **Webber,** *The Coming of the Warrior-King*, p. 59.

2 **Canon Dr Brian Meardon,** in a personal letter of 10 August 2007.

Chapter 3

1 **Webber,** *The Coming of the Warrior-King*, p. 66.

Chapter 6

1 **Baker,** *Nahum, Habakkuk and Zephaniah*, p. 104.

2 **David Hewetson,** *Zephaniah: Bible Probe* (Homebush West, NSW: Anzea Books, 1981), p. 36.

3 **Theo Laetsch,** *The Minor Prophets* (St Louis, MO: Concordia, 1956), p. 371.

4 **Baker,** *Nahum, Habakkuk and Zephaniah*, p. 108.

Chapter 7

1 **Percy Bysshe Shelley,** 'Ozymandias', *The New Oxford Book of English Verse*, ed. Helen Gardner (OUP, 1973), p. 580.

2 **Webber,** *The Coming of the Warrior-King*, p. 144.

3 **Michael Bentley,** *Balancing the Books: Micah and Nahum simply explained* (Welwyn: Evangelical Press, 1994), p. 106.

Chapter 8

1 **John Calvin,** *Commentaries on the Minor Prophets* (Grand Rapids, MI: Baker, n.d.), p. 390.

2 **J. Vernon McGee,** *Commentary #31: Zephaniah and Haggai* (Pasadena, CA: Thru the Bible Books, 1979), p. 47.

3 **Laetsch,** *The Minor Prophets*, p. 375.

Chapter 9

1 **Thomas O. Chisholm,** 'Great is thy faithfulness', 1923.

2 **John Keble,** 'New every morning is the love', 1827.

Chapter 10

1 Both quotations are from **John Blanchard,** *Gathered Gold* (Darlington: Evangelical Press, 1984), pp. 299–300.

2 **Anthony Selvaggio,** *The Prophets Speak of Him* (Darlington: Evangelical Press, 2006), p. 132.

Chapter 11

1 **Gilley,** *This Little Church*, p. 68.

2 **Robert Hawker,** *Commentary on the Holy Bible* (London: Sherwood, Neeley and Jones, 1822), vol. 6, p. 476.

3 Confession 21 (Evening Prayer) from *Common Worship* (London: Church House Publishing, 2006).

4 **Graham Kendrick,** 'My Lord, what love is this', 1989.

Chapter 12

1 **Bentley,** *Balancing the Books*, p. 58.

2 **Webber,** *The Coming of the Warrior-King*, p. 179.

3 **Albert E. Brumley,** 'This world is not my home', 1965.

About Day One:

Day One's threefold commitment:

- To be faithful to the Bible, God's inerrant, infallible Word;
- To be relevant to our modern generation;
- To be excellent in our publication standards.

I continue to be thankful for the publications of Day One. They are biblical; they have sound theology; and they are relative to the issues at hand. The material is condensed and manageable while, at the same time, being complete—a challenging balance to find. We are happy in our ministry to make use of these excellent publications.

JOHN MACARTHUR, PASTOR-TEACHER, GRACE COMMUNITY CHURCH, CALIFORNIA

It is a great encouragement to see Day One making such excellent progress. Their publications are always biblical, accessible and attractively produced, with no compromise on quality. Long may their progress continue and increase!

JOHN BLANCHARD, AUTHOR, EVANGELIST AND APOLOGIST

Visit our website for more information and to request a free catalogue of our books.

www.dayone.co.uk

Opening up series

Title	Author	ISBN
Opening up 1 Corinthians	Derek Prime	978–1–84625–004–0
Opening up 1 Thessalonians	Tim Shenton	978–1–84625–031–6
Opening up 1 Timothy	Simon J Robinson	978–1–903087–69–5
Opening up 2 & 3 John	Terence Peter Crosby	978–1–84625–023–1
Opening up 2 Peter	Clive Anderson	978–1–84625–077–4
Opening up 2 Thessalonians (in preparation)	Ian McNaughton	978–1–84625–117–7
Opening up 2 Timothy	Peter Williams	978–1–84625–065–1
Opening up Amos	Michael Bentley	978–1–84625–041–5
Opening up Colossians & Philemon	Ian McNaughton	978–1–84625–016–3
Opening up Ecclesiastes	Jim Winter	978–1–903087–86–2
Opening up Exodus	Iain D Campbell	978–1–84625–029–3
Opening up Ezekiel's visions	Peter Jeffery	978–1–903087–66–4
Opening up Ezra	Peter Williams	978–1–84625–022–4
Opening up Hebrews	Philip Hacking	978–1–84625–042–2
Opening up Jonah	Paul Mackrell	978–1–84625–080–4

108